BREAKING TRADITION

AN EXPLORATION
OF THE
HISTORICAL RELATIONSHIP
BETWEEN
THEORY and PRACTICE
IN
SECOND LANGUAGE
TEACHING

The McGraw-Hill Second Language Professional Series

(FORMERLY "THE MCGRAW-HILL FOREIGN LANGUAGE PROFESSIONAL SERIES")

General Editors: James F. Lee and Bill VanPatten

Directions in Second Language Learning

(FORMERLY "DIRECTIONS FOR LANGUAGE LEARNING AND TEACHING")

Primarily for students of second language acquisition and teaching, curriculum developers, and teacher educators, *Directions in Second Language Learning* explores how languages are learned and used and how knowledge about language acquisition and use informs language teaching. The books in this strand emphasize principled approaches to language classroom instruction and management as well as to the education of foreign and second language teachers.

Beyond Methods: Components of Second Language Teacher Education. Edited by Kathleen Bardovi-Harlig and Beverly Hartford (both of Indiana University)
Order number: 0-07-006106-8

Communicative Competence: Theory and Classroom Practice, Second Edition, by Sandra J. Savignon (The Pennsylvania State University)
Order number: 0-07-083736-8

Making Communicative Language Teaching Happen, by James F. Lee and Bill VanPatten (both of University of Illinois, Urbana-Champaign)
Order number: 0-07-037693-x

Workbook to accompany *Making Communicative Language Teaching Happen*, by James F. Lee and Bill VanPatten
Order number: 0-07-083736-8

Perspectives on Theory and Research

Primarily for scholars and researchers of second language acquisition and teaching, *Perspectives on Theory and Research* seeks to advance knowledge about the nature of language learning in and out of the classroom by offering current research on language learning and teaching from diverse perspectives and frameworks.

Breaking Tradition: An Exploration of the Historical Relationship between Theory and Practice in Second Language Teaching, by Diane Musumeci (University of Illinois, Urbana-Champaign)
Order number: 0-07-044394-7

BREAKING TRADITION

AN EXPLORATION
OF THE
HISTORICAL RELATIONSHIP
BETWEEN
THEORY and PRACTICE
IN
SECOND LANGUAGE
TEACHING

DIANE MUSUMECI

UNIVERSITY OF ILLINOIS, URBANA-CHAMPAIGN

The McGraw-Hill Companies, Inc.

New York   St. Louis   San Francisco   Auckland   Bogotá   Caracas   Lisbon
London   Madrid   Mexico City   Milan   Montreal   New Delhi   San Juan
Singapore   Sydney   Tokyo   Toronto

A Division of The McGraw·Hill Companies

This is an ⎝Đ⎠ book.

This book was set in Palatino by The Clarinda Company
The editors were Thalia Dorwick and Gregory Trauth.
The production supervisor was Michelle Lyon.
R.R. Donnelley & Sons was printer and binder.

Library of Congress Cataloging-in-Publication Data
Musumeci, Diane.
    Breaking tradition : an exploration of the historical relationship
between theory and practice in second language teaching / Diane
Musumeci.
        p.   cm. — (The McGraw-Hill second language professional
series / perspectives on theory and research)
    Includes bibliographical references and index.
    ISBN 0-07-044394-7
    1.   English language—Study and teaching—Foreign speakers—Theory,
etc.   2.   Latin language, Medieval and modern—Study and teaching—
History.   3.   Language and languages—Study and teaching—Theory,
etc.   4.   Communication, International—History.   5.   Second language
acquisition—History.   6.   Education, Humanistic—History.
I. Title.   II. Series
PE1128.A2M88   1997
428'.007—dc21   96-46729
                                                                           CIP

http://www.mhcollege.com

ABOUT THE AUTHOR

Diane Musumeci is Associate Professor of Italian and S.L.A.T.E. (Second Language Acquisition and Teacher Education) at the University of Illinois at Urbana-Champaign, where she is Director of Basic Language Instruction in Italian. She received her Ph.D. in Italian linguistics with a Certificate of Advanced Study in S.L.A.T.E. from the University of Illinois at Urbana-Champaign in 1989. She conducts research in content-based instruction and classroom language acquistion. She teaches a wide range of courses from first semester Italian to doctoral seminars on the histroy of second language teaching. She has published numerous articles and chapters in books and is the author of *Il carciofo: Strategie di lettura e proposte d'attività* (McGraw-Hill, 1990).

CREDITS

Grateful acknowledgment is made for the use of the following illustrations:

Page 9: Guarino Veronese in a portrait on parchment, Trivulziana Library (photo: Saporetti, Milan)

Page 35: Ignatius of Loyola pen sketch modeled on 1584 portrait by Alonzo Sanches Coello from *Saint Ignatius' Idea of a Jesuit University* by George Ganse (Milwaukee: Marquette University Press, 1954)

Page 71: J.A. Comenius from *The Great Didactic of John Amos Comenius* by M.W. Keatinge, M.A. (London: Adam and Charles Black, 1910)

Page 81: The inward parts of a city from *Orbis sensualism pictus* by John Comenius, 1672

CONTENTS

The discovery of classical texts in the Renaissance causes an explosion of interest in ancient culture and knowledge. Fluency in the Latin language is the key to access this intellectual wealth, and Latin reigns as the international language of politics, scholarship, and commerce. In response to the need to simultaneously develop functional competence in Latin and in a wide range of subject areas, the early humanists create private schools that offer a radically new curriculum: the humanities. Guarino Guarini's school is particularly successful; he earns a reputation as one of the greatest language teachers of all time. His son, Battista, attempts to document his father's methodology for future generations, but the final product fails to capture Guarino's vision.

Middle-class families clamor to share in the prestige and career opportunities afforded by knowledge of Latin. Ignatius of Loyola devises a system of education that makes the study of humanities available to all boys, those who aspire to become leaders in the political arena or the business community, as well as those who seek membership in the Jesuit order. However, when Ignatius's design is converted into a detailed plan for the management of these schools, a struggle develops between the proponents of a uniform classroom pedagogy and the goals of the humanities-based curriculum.

A technological breakthrough, the printing press, along with the expansion of Protestantism, facilitates the spread of public schools. Johann Amos Comenius writes a hugely popular language textbook for school children that is adopted throughout Europe. The humanities, however, become suspect as appropriate subject matter for children, and Latin gives way to the vernacular as the language of instruction.

The rise of a new world language, English, sets in motion a replay of the early humanists' arguments for the reform of language teaching methodology — now known as communicative language teaching. Can the successes and failures of the past inform current discussions regarding the use of the L2 as the medium of instruction, the role of grammar, and the emphasis on content over form?

FOREWORD

The word "tradition" evokes concepts such as "time-honored" and "long-standing." In *Breaking Tradition*, Diane Musumeci rightfully questions the short memory span that characterizes the field of language teaching. When today's language instructors speak of "traditional" teaching methods, they are often referring to the Audiolingual Methodology, an approach to structuring language materials and practice that was developed in post-World War II military schools. There is a rich history of language teaching, however, that predates the mid-twentieth century, a history that Musumeci illuminates in her treatise. Educators of the 15th, 16th, and 17th centuries were just as concerned as we are today about the role of grammar in learning, the place of literary works in a language curriculum, the use of the target language as the medium of instruction rather than the object of instruction, and the content of language learning.

Musumeci's exploration of the past is a fascinating account of how theory has been repeatedly mistranslated into practice. First, she establishes for us a tradition of language teaching that is, without doubt, communicatively oriented. Musumeci examines the works of Guarino Guarini, a 15th century educator, and Ignatius of Loyola, a 16th century educational administrator, as they wrote about the teaching of Latin, very much a spoken world language in their day. She demonstrates how the tradition these innovators and theorists adhered to was broken by their followers. In the case of Guarino, his son penned a treatise that proclaimed that his writings were faithful to his father's thoughts, philosophies, and practices. Yet Musumeci's juxtapositions of the father's letters with the son's prescriptions for language instruction reveal significant contradictions. In the case of Ignatius of Loyola, his followers also penned a treatise, claiming that it codified the teachings of Ignatius, and then required the ever-expanding Jesuit schools to adhere strictly to the prescriptions set out in their treatise. Again, Musumeci adeptly compares the original writings of Ignatius with their subsequent interpretations, demonstrating the contradictions between Loyola's teachings and their implementation in the schools. She then examines the writings of Comenius, a 17th century educational innovator, who advocated teaching large numbers of children in the same classroom and who introduced illustrations into textbooks. Musumeci shows Comenius's own writings to be a series of contradictions between his statements on how learning and teaching happen in theory and his recommendations for actual classroom practice.

The closing chapter of *Breaking Tradition* takes us into contemporary times. Musumeci's analysis of contemporary writings exposes further inconsistencies between theory and practice. As a discipline, language teaching has an apparent tradition of not conveying theory into practice; Musumeci argues persuasively that this tradition can be broken. Often, tradition is evoked as the rationale for not undertaking critical examination or subsequent innovation. Yet breaking open what we adhere to as tradition and examining it critically could yield fascinating results.

Breaking Tradition is a valuable addition to scholarship, a "must read" for anyone who hopes to understand the ever-present tension between theory and practice in language instruction.

J.F.L.
B.VP.

ACKNOWLEDGMENTS

It is common for authors to list people to whom they are particularly indebted for their respective contributions to the project being published. I, too, am sincerely grateful to many colleagues whom I admire and whose friendship and collegiality have and continue to sustain me in my work. However, in all honesty, they were not the ones who motivated me to conduct this particular research.

Instead, I would like to thank the many unnamed colleagues and students who inpired me to write this book:

- those who, while cleaning out files, threw away everything dated prior to 1975 because it was "irrelevant" to the field of second language acquisition and contemporary language teaching practice;
- those who dismissed "humanism" as the pop psychology of the 1970's, or worse, a threat to traditional moral values;
- those who insisted that languages are best taught through grammar and translation because "that's the way it's always been";
- and those who, in my graduate seminar on the history of second language teaching, upon reading an 18th-century account of an early-level second language class, exclaimed, "Hey! I could do this with my students tomorrow!"

I would also like to acknowledge publicly that I am very much a product of my environment: This work was greatly facilitated by the University of Illinois at Urbana-Champaign with its atmosphere of intellectual curiosity, continual stimulus for research, remarkable tolerance for experimentation and interdisciplinary work, and a library that spoils us rotten.

Finally, a few names must be mentioned: First, Jim Lee and Bill Van-Patten, the series editors, who are dear friends and esteemed colleagues and who make work in our department—in the words of Guarino—"pleasant, welcome, fruitful, and fertile;" second, Sandra Savignon and Margie Berns, who first encouraged me to widen my own perspective on language teaching—it marked the beginning of a fascinating adventure; and, finally, Antonino, Gian-Paolo, Nick, and Wally who remind me daily to have a life.

D.M., Champaign, IL, December 1996

Si qua forte vera et fidei nostrae accomo-
data scriptores dixerunt, non solum formi-
danda non sunt, sed ab eis etiam tanquam
ab iniustis possessoribus in usum nos-
trum vendicanda.

[If sometimes the Ancient Authors make
claims that are in harmony with our
beliefs, then not only shouldn't we be
afraid, but we should take them over as
our own, as if they weren't in the right
hands to begin with.]
—Augustine, *On Christian Doctrine* II, 61.
quoted by Guarino Guarini in his letter to
Friar Giovanni da Prato, 1450

Tradition and Language Teaching

> *Nescire autem quid ante quam natus sis acciderit, id est semper esse puerum. Quid enim est aetas hominis, nisi ea memoria rerum veterum cum superiorum aetate contexitur?*
>
> [But to be ignorant of what happened before you were born, that is the same as always being a child. For what does "age" mean for a person, if it is not interwoven with the age of past generations through knowledge of the history of ancient times?]
> —Marcus Tullius Cicero,
> *Orator* 34.120, 55 B.C.

Applied linguistics and dinosaurs have something in common: They both once ruled the earth; they became extinct; and they are presently enjoying a revival, which apparently has something to do with DNA. Yet while most ten-year-olds can rattle off the names of at least five dinosaurs that roamed the earth over 65 million years ago and can tell you two theories of how they became extinct, many applied linguists would be hard pressed to do the same for their profession. Although we make reference to "traditional" language teaching, with the assumption that everyone knows what the term means, only a handful of studies have examined systematically how language teaching has evolved over the past two thousand years.

A discussion of tradition—or its flipside, innovation—first requires an acknowledgment of its deictic nature; that is, whether we identify an event as an *innovation* rather than as a *tradition* depends in large part on our perspective. Some people view change primarily in a positive light: it represents

1

progress, improvement, enlightenment, and relevance. Those who embrace innovation as a desirable force may interpret tradition on the contrary as stasis, stagnation, or old-fashionedness. Teachers who identify themselves with this group may flock to conferences and workshops, looking forward to learning different ways of doing things. They anticipate with excitement the arrival of the latest textbooks and materials. Subsequently, they are sometimes disappointed and frustrated when, in the classroom, those activities and textbooks do not meet with great success. They find that the new materials are not, in practice, much different from what they had used before, or they drop the materials in here and there, adding to or subtracting from their bags of tricks that work, but without much thought as to why.

For others, change is largely negative: it stands for chaos, uncertainty, trendiness, or the unproved. This group confronts flux with trepidation and cynicism, preferring to maintain the comfort of the status quo, sticking with the "tried and true." They eye innovation with a healthy skepticism. These language teachers peruse the freshly-minted textbooks replete with "new" activities only to discover that they've been doing them that way for years. They are, in turn, reassured that their classroom practices have been validated once again; however, they may be a little disconcerted and frustrated by the fact that there really isn't anything new under the sun in second language teaching.

These represent the two extremes of personal reaction to innovation. Of course, most of us probably fall somewhere in between, our curiosities piqued by the latest theories of language learning and yet somewhat at a loss as to what they mean for language teaching. By and large, we teach languages the way we were taught them, or we follow a particular book or method that we discovered in some teacher training course. Or at least we think we do.

Whether we welcome variation or avoid it, the perspective of a single individual is, by necessity, extremely narrow; it is limited by one's personal experience. Therefore, we have no way of distinguishing between the "new" and the "tried and true." We have come to call "traditional" what one has always done, and "innovative" what one has never experienced before.

This research takes a broader, historical perspective. It investigates the tradition of both theory and practice in applied linguistics over the course of three centuries, as represented by three major participants in the debate. It looks at the beliefs held by educational reformers who wanted to change the way second languages were taught, and it examines how their theories of language learning were communicated to the language teaching profession and what happened in that process. The examination of the historical relationship between ideas about how second languages are learned (i.e., theory) and methodologies for how they are taught (i.e., practice) reveals interesting patterns in the history of second language teaching. It is a discovery that calls for a reinterpretation of what constitutes "traditional" language teaching and, at the same time, provides a model for the vicissitudinous journey from vision to implementation.

Since the early 1970s, fueled in part by first language acquisition research and the argument that language acquisition is largely an innate human capacity, and in part by an escalating global economy in a multilingual workplace, interest in second language learning has been burgeoning. Each year researchers publish an exponentially increasing number of studies on second language acquisition; publishers produce a flurry of second and foreign language textbooks promoted as either "new" and "latest" or "proved" and "solid;" and the language teaching profession at large is deluged with books on how languages are learned and the best way to teach them.

Across all perspectives—whether teacher, researcher, administrator, or textbook author—the essential questions and concerns are remarkably the same: Should grammar rules be taught? How should errors be corrected? What role does comprehension play in second language acquisition? Is exposure to comprehensible L2 sufficient for acquisition to occur or must it be accompanied by instruction and/or interaction? How much of second language acquisition is universally determined and how much depends upon the characteristics of the individual learner?

Applied linguists attempt to answer these concerns. Researchers relate the findings of their latest studies, replete with tables, graphics, and statistics, providing evidence in support of a particular theory of second language acquisition. Textbook publishers, in turn, use research findings and market surveys to entice teachers with materials and technologies that loudly and assuredly promise "mastery," "fluency," or "proficiency." Methodologists promote or dispute the effectiveness of myriad teaching practices. It is not surprising that conflicting research findings and opposing methodological stances exist side by side. In fact, the one point on which almost everyone agrees is that scant evidence exists to support any single, unified theory of language learning, let alone of language teaching. Therefore, language teachers are left on their own to make sense of the research, pedagogical advice, and textbooks, and then must consolidate them in their own classroom practices.

Although they agree that much more needs to be known about how second languages are acquired, language professionals are limited in their recommendations for remediation. Additional studies need to be done, such as large-scale studies, case studies, cross-linguistic studies, longitudinal studies, descriptive studies, and studies on the actual effects of proposed changes in classroom practices. The list goes on and on. In an effort to amass data and inform teaching practice, some applied linguists even advocate that classroom teachers themselves take active roles as researchers, in addition to their regular teaching responsibilities. However, one kind of study remains portentously missing from the research agenda: the historical study. The questions facing today's second language teaching profession are fascinating, but have they never been asked before? The research agenda is exciting, but with barely thirty years of data accumulated so far, also daunting. Is it possible that more than two thousand years of language learning and teaching have nothing to contribute to the discussion?

Based on what one reads in the current literature, it appears almost as though language learning were an exclusively twentieth-century phenomenon, unparalleled throughout history, a heretofore terra incognita that can only be explored by today's applied linguists, armed with the latest technologic tools and research designs. With due deference to the many second language acquisition specialists who are conducting worthwhile, necessary research with sometimes fascinating results, what remains missing from the data are the voices from the past: wise voices of teachers and scholars who participated in one of the most wide-scale foreign language experiments ever. Through their eyes applied linguistics experienced the growth and decline of the first true world language, Latin, while barbarians were still babbling the gibberish that would become the second, English.

The lack of interest surrounding what language teaching looked like prior to the latter half of the twentieth century is puzzling. Is our past kept secret because it was dismal? Is our professional closet filled with pedagogical skeletons? Or is it perhaps counterproductive to applied linguistics—a field that has assumed the role of "new kid on the block" in so-called "traditional" language departments—to acknowledge that it even has a history, let alone one that parallels the study of literature?

When it is referenced in research articles or pedagogical manuals, the history of language teaching is commonly described as a linear progression from behaviorism (notably, audiolingualism in the United States) to communicative language teaching. Other accounts refer to various "direct" methods (i.e., the Direct Method, the Cleveland Method, and, in its most recent incarnation, the Natural Approach), as opposed to "cognitive" methods and a smattering of colorful, highly stylized, but marginally accepted methods (i.e., Community Language Learning, Suggestopedia, the Silent Way, and the Dartmouth Method). Significantly, this profusion of methods appears in the literature post-1930. Everything prior to that date is referred to as either "grammar translation" or "traditional" language teaching. Those concerned with second language acquisition and teaching are left with the impression that: (1) second language teaching prior to the twentieth century was minimal and monolithic in scope and practice; and (2) either issues concerning grammar, errors, input, and so forth were inapplicable throughout the long history of the profession or our predecessors' primitive treatment of those concerns is irrelevant in modern context.

Language professionals who participate in or otherwise react to the current barrage of research findings, teaching manuals, and language textbooks, equipped with only a sketchy understanding of the history of language teaching, are at a distinct disadvantage. They are limited in their ability to critically assess theory, research findings, or methodologic approaches because they can neither evaluate the "state-of-the-art" outside the present nor envision its place in the larger historical context. Deprived of the wisdom that the measure of time and historical perspective affords, these professionals are blind to the difference between the ephemeral and the durable, between the gimmicky and the effective. Unaware of the failures and accomplishments of the past in their own profession, these language professionals are found to repeat the former and to struggle needlessly toward the latter.

The following two examples are far flung, but represent not uncommon responses to the outpouring of information on second language acquisition. A graduate student in applied linguistics recently asked if it would be acceptable to cite a research study conducted in the late 1970s, or if such research should be considered obsolete. It seems that in her other courses the references given were all less than five years old. At the opposite extreme, during a workshop on communicative language teaching for language teachers, a teacher with more than twenty years of classroom experience dismissed as faddish the presenter's suggestion to use activities that require students to focus on the meaning of a message instead of using pattern drills. In the first instance, a knowledge of language teaching's history could have provided insight that the graduate student needed to interpret the significance of the 1979 article in the current debates surrounding language learning and teaching. In the second example, an awareness of past practices and results would have allowed the teacher to assess which, if any, of the proposed changes in classroom practice would be truly experimental and which would actually represent a return to time-honored practices.

Ultimately, the advantage of taking a historical look at beliefs about language learning and how they evolved is that such an approach allows for an appraisal of the profession from the vantage point of temporal distance. In doing so, it permits the discernment of both dramatic shifts and enduring trends. It provides a panoramic view of the profession's evolutionary landscape: that is, of the forest, not just of the trees.

In 1983, in a volume entitled *Fundamental Concepts of Language Teaching*, H. H. Stern devotes an entire chapter to plead in favor of historical research, stating with commiseration that "language teaching theory has a short memory" and that it suffers from a lack of "historical depth" (pp. 76–77). More recently, Brumfit and Mitchell (1990) argue that language teaching benefits from research conducted from a variety of disciplinary perspectives: psycholinguistic, sociolinguistic, anthropological, *and* historical. Notwithstanding arguments that propose the important contribution that historical research can make to second language education, a review of recent publications in applied linguistics reveals no titles that espouse a historical approach. The standard text on the history of second language teaching remains Kelly's 1969 volume entitled *25 Centuries of Language Teaching*. As the title indicates, the author attempts to provide a historical overview of second language teaching practice. Although it contains an impressive number of citations from multiple sources and centuries, the compendious nature of Kelly's work precludes an in-depth analysis of particular movements or beliefs about language learning.

In contrast to Kelley's thematic approach, two books instead examine the history of language teaching from a chronological perspective. Mackey (1965) describes in a few pages the evolution of language teaching from antiquity to modern times before proceeding to the core of his argument: the development of a model for the analysis of practice. Beginning with the Renaissance, Titone (1968) provides a less rapid, but still broad historical overview before he focuses on the debate between formalism and activism during the late nineteenth and early twentieth centuries. It should be remembered that Mackey, Titone, and especially Kelly are products of the heyday of audiolingualism, a bias that patently permeates their research.

In addition to these historical summaries of language teaching methodologies, books also deal only with English and its language teaching history, or treat a particular language during a specific time period (e.g., French during the sixteenth century). Although interesting in their own right, these books examine language teaching as practice, not as theory. As such, although they provide detailed descriptions of schools, enrollment figures, textbooks, and curricula, these books do not probe the underlying beliefs about how languages are learned.

To reiterate, the present study intends to investigate the relationship between second language teaching theory and guidelines for teaching practice. A diachronic rather than a synchronic approach is used in order to tap language teaching's rich history and to document the enduring consistencies in beliefs and changes in practice.

In order to illuminate what has meant, historically, to know a second language and what those expectations have implied for teaching, this study looks at the writings of three educators who are also proponents of pedagogical reforms: Guarino Guarini (1374–1460), Ignatius of Loyola (1491–1556), and Johannes Amos Comenius (1592–1670). These men were chosen for two reasons: They are among the most influential figures in the history of Western education, and they were all practitioners (i.e., veteran language teachers and/or administrators) not solely philosophers. Thus, it is reasonable to presume that the beliefs that they held about language learning and teaching were formed by their classroom experiences, with real students and teachers. The changes that they advocated in the areas of curriculum, school organization, and pedagogical materials profoundly affected the teaching of what was the universal language of scholarship, education, government, and the marketplace throughout the Western world for approximately two thousand years, namely Latin. In fact, they continue to form the basis for language teaching practice today.

Even though these three reformers are featured in every comprehensive history of Western education, this research differs from that found in general educational texts because it focuses specifically on the educators' beliefs regarding the learning and teaching of a second language, rather than on broad pedagogical principles.

Readers will find that the three educators in question are quoted extensively. The use of longer citations is essential to this research for a number of reasons. First, it is assumed that the readers are not familiar with the texts and would benefit from their ready availability. Second, the writings of the educators constitute the actual data; they comprise the only evidence available from which to reconstruct their theories. Third, the argument will be made that the theories underwent fundamental revisions as they were put into practice. Therefore, it is important that the readers have direct access to the original sources so that they may evaluate for themselves the strength of the argument. Finally, it is hoped that readers will find these forthright voices of the past delightfully refreshing!

This study is predicated upon the premise that a less narrow approach to second language studies—one that includes a historical perspective on second language teaching—can only benefit the field of applied linguistics. It would expand the available database to researchers, grant access to a large body of previously ignored evidence about second language learning and teaching, and provide the benefits of a longitudinal perspective. To the language program administrator, it offers insight into the relationship between change, curricula, and teacher education. Such awareness may help to explain why "innovative" language programs are difficult to establish and maintain. For the language teacher, it provides a framework for the interpretation and evaluation of research findings and methodology for classroom practice.

The history of second language teaching has received short shrift in current applied linguistics and second language teacher education programs. This book attempts to remedy that situation by presenting the views of some of the most respected and influential figures of the profession's past. In doing so, it also reveals historical constancy in language teaching theory as well as impediments to innovation in teaching practice. To appreciate the tradition and how it has been, and continues to be, transmitted are essential to understanding our contribution to the academe.

Pause to consider . . .

Stern's (1983) suggestion that a historical approach to language teaching begins with teachers' personal histories. How similar are your classroom practices to those of your former teachers? What have you preserved from past experience? Materials? Techniques? Management style? Why?

The Teacher: Innovation in the Curriculum

Guarino Guarini   (1374–1460)

*I will propose briefly, Prince Lionello,
some rules, a kind of method, that I
learned from Manuele Chrysoloras, my
teacher of virtue and doctrine, while he
was my guide on the path of letters.
First of all, you must read [...] Don't
go word by word, rather pay attention
only to the meaning, and as though
you were trying to grab a body not an
appendage.*

—Guarino Guarini,
Letter to Lionello d'Este, 1434

*In teaching, the fact that verb tenses
are formed according to a general rule
is of utmost importance [...] To such an
extent that (this is extremely useful in
that language) in the blink of an eye
they can distinguish a noun from a
verb and the tenses of the verbs. They
will soon arrive at the point where they
can respond accurately to frequent
interrogations by the teacher. Then, little by little, they will come in contact
with the [ancient] authors, starting
with the easiest prose writers because
you don't want to wear them out by
the profundity of the content at the
expense of practicing the rules that
they have learned. [The rules], first and
foremost, are what we consider the
most important thing of all.*

—Battista Guarino,
*The Program of Teaching and
Learning, 1459*

"Scientists Discover Life on Mars." Imagine the headline. Now suppose that the Martians are highly intelligent beings with a civilization that far surpasses anything on Earth. They have a system of government that is more rational and fair: All citizens are well-educated; women ordinarily hold positions of honor and prestige; their cities are beautifully designed; the arts flourish; crime is nonexistent; and they have outpaced us in medicine and science. Think how eager we would be to learn everything we could about them: their clothing, their music, their language. If you can envision all of this, you can begin to understand how the discovery of ancient Greece and Rome affected European intellectuals during the fifteenth century.

The rediscovery of the classics during the Renaissance resulted in more than an information explosion in academia; it constituted the renewal of a love affair between education and the cultures of ancient Greece and Rome. Certainly, comparisons of ancient manuscripts with incomplete and botched medieval copies or translations revealed the linguistic mutations that had transpired and that philologists were anxious to correct. Fluency in Latin, however, represented much more than the ability to edit manuscripts. Learning Latin was not an aesthetic endeavor for its own sake, the "in" thing to do. It was a language of considerable usefulness as the language of culture and international communication, and therefore power. In other words, learning Latin in the fifteenth century was not very different from learning English today, in the age of the Global Village.

In terms of education, the revival of interest sparked by the newly available classical works undermined the medieval curriculum's focus on rules of grammar and logical argumentation, dialectics. A new curriculum was proposed, the *studia humanitatis* (literally, study of humanity). In the words of the Latin secretary to Leo X, Cardinal Giacomo Sadoleto, this innovation provides a program that makes students both "wise and moral."

THE STUDIA HUMANITATIS

Vergerius, a Latin scholar of the time and an eminent proponent of the *studia humanitatis*, describes in great detail the new program of learning. His treatise, entitled *De ingenuis moribus et liberalibus studiis* [*On the Conduct and Education of Young People*], was one of the most widely read productions of the Renaissance for 150 years after its appearance around 1400. In it, literature, to be understood in general as the reading of books, plays a dominant role. In a time when Latin and Greek manuscripts were discovered almost daily, it is not surprising that the humanists—as the enthusiasts of the new learning are called—advocate a curriculum based on texts. Vergerius states that books are the key element in the curriculum because they "exhibit not facts alone, but thoughts, and their expression" (from *De ingenuis moribus et liberalibus studiis; On the Conduct and Education of Young People*; in the translation by Woodward 1921, p. 105). Next, he outlines the specific areas of study to include in the curriculum and why.

The first subject to be studied is history, accompanied by moral philosophy. According to the scholar, history is intrinsically interesting for young people. Furthermore, it supplies "concrete examples of the precepts inculcated by philosophy; the one shows what men should do, the other what men have said and done in the past" (p. 106). Next, the curriculum must include eloquence, or speaking ability in Latin. Vergerius states that whereas "by philosophy we learn the essential truth of things," eloquence allows us to persuade others of that truth (p. 106). Grammar, or the "art of letters," is the third subject in Vergerius's list (p. 107). It does not refer to the study of rules as we might understand "grammar" today; instead, it refers to the act of writing and composition. According to Vergerius, letters provide "the foundation on which the whole study of literature must rest." He asserts that if students are to derive profit from what they study, they must pay attention to the way they convey their ideas to others: using discourse appropriate to the intended audience, clear argumentation, and accuracy in expressing their thoughts (p. 107). "Letters," then, is the written equivalent of eloquence, and it includes disputation, or logical argumentation, to enable students to discern fallacy from truth in discussion (p. 107). The art of public speaking is considered a civil science, important for the public citizen. Therefore, rhetoric, which included oration, forms another part of the *studia humanitatis*. The curriculum also offers poetry for leisure and music as a healthy form of recreation. Arithmetic and geometry are incorporated into the program because they possess "a peculiar element of certainty" (p. 108). Finally, science is recommended because it imparts knowledge of natural phenomena. The study of nature leads to fascinating investigations because it deals with "the explanation of their wonders by the unraveling of their causes" (p. 108).

Along with naming these subjects, Vergerius also suggests how they should be studied. He recognizes that mental endowments differ, and that students' abilities determine the subjects in which they excel. Nevertheless, he insists that all students benefit from the following practices. They should review every evening what they have heard and read during the day to assimilate and integrate information. Talking with other students about what they are studying is very beneficial: It would aid in expression, understanding, and remembering. They should attempt to explain the material to someone else as a way to teach what they had learned, an ideal way to better grasp it themselves. But above all, they would have to read. Vergerius recommended that everyone "give a fixed time each day to reading, which shall be encroached upon under no pretext whatsoever" (p. 112).

The innovation in the curriculum that the *studia humanitatis* represented involves more than the addition of new subjects to an existent educational program. Instead, the goal of learning Latin shifted from the preparation of students who could accurately copy manuscripts or compose in imitation of classical authors to the study of what those authors had to say, in Latin. Far from imparting an aesthetic appreciation alone, the revival of learning was proposed as a practical education. With its emphasis on the study of Latin history, philosophy, and science, it sought to give students the background that would allow them to replicate the best patrimony of ancient Greece and Rome. It would provide models of government and erudition. Students would be able to access advances in science that had been lost. The humanities were intended as a course of study whose function was the formation of good citizens. Reading the Latin authors was not simply a way of learning a language, but how one gained access to information necessary for personal, moral, and civic development (Garin 1958, p. XXVII).

---

*P*ause to consider . . .

the role of humanities in the present-day university. Which subjects are required as part of everyone's general education, regardless of major? What contemporary purpose does the study of humanities serve? Does it make better citizens?

GUARINO GUARINI
AND THE STUDIA HUMANITATIS

Among the most celebrated proponents of the *studia humanitatis* was Guarino Guarini (1374-1460), also known as Guarino Veronese, an early humanist of the Italian Renaissance. Born in 1374 in Verona, son of a homemaker and a metal smith, Guarino studied under several important scholars. He eventually became associated with the only Greek scholar in Italy at the time, Manuele Chrysoloras. Because a knowledge of Greek, along with Latin, was essential for the scholar who wanted to read classical authors, Guarino became an avid pupil of Chrysoloras, and he was the first of the young Italian humanists to go to Byzantium to "perfect his culture" (Cecchi & Sapegno 1966, p. 125). Upon his return to Italy, Guarino was welcomed as a teacher and scholar in both classical languages. He traveled throughout northern Italy as a public and private teacher of Greek and Latin, a translator of texts both literary and nonliterary, a respected advisor for methods of teaching and conducting research, and a proponent of school reform. In 1429, Guarino was engaged as the teacher of Lionello d'Este, prince of Ferrara, and in 1442 he inaugurated his own public school in the same city. He died in 1460, at age 86, renowned throughout Europe for his efficacy as a teacher of Latin and Greek, as evidenced by the accomplishments of his many and illustrious pupils.

Guarino's stance regarding the value of the *studia humanitatis* is apparent in the following letter. In it, he congratulates Cristoforo Sabbion, the chancellor of Verona, on his decision to pursue the new course of learning, with the assurance that "There is nothing better, nothing more useful, nothing more pleasant that you could do for the present age or the future. With the study of letters [*studia humanitatis*] one can attain the best manner of living, gather important information, and enjoy rare pleasures" (in Garin, pp. 322-324, all translations mine). Later in the same letter, Guarino offers an assessment of the current cultural situation, lamenting:

> Today education has vanished, culture is despised, studies disdained. And I'm not talking only about the common person; but what of the prince, the king, the emperor who, through his ignorance of letters, you would have to number among the uncouth and barbarous. They are called gentlemen-lords, not because they have distinguished themselves in letters and fine arts, but because, by circumstance of luck, they boast the right to be more licentious, lazier, greedier, more lethargic [than others]. (pp. 322-324)

The new curriculum that Guarino envisions as capable of correcting such cultural stagnation is not intended only for the future teacher-scholar. The *studia humanitatis* were considered essential in the formative education of all citizens, especially those who would be in positions of authority. In a letter to Giovanni Nicola Salerno di Dolceto, Guarino reminds the politician of the value of his humanistic training and of the responsibility inherent in his position to foster the same kind of learning among the next generation of leaders:

> You owe a great deal to the Muses, under whose sign you were trained and raised from childhood; you learned to make your way, to govern, to strengthen and sustain yourself, your family, and the affairs of citizens. And, so, it's up to you to show that the Muses aren't only teachers of harmony and the lute, but also of political strategy and art [because] if a leader is just, good, prudent, and modest (all virtues deriving from letters and arts), then those virtues will be spread among all the people (p. 328).

Likewise, in his letter accompanying the gift of his translation of Plutarch's book on the difference between a flatterer and a friend, Guarino reminds Lionello d'Este, former pupil and now King of Ferrara, of his obligation as a leader to act as a model for his followers:

> This little gift, o great Lionello, my most benevolent king, is offered under the guise of Plutarch by your Guarino, and if I notice that you have enjoyed it, it will push me to find other subjects of study. [...] And our young people, encouraged by your judgment [that the reading of literature is worthwhile], will be more apt to read and to profit by reading. We see that people are such that they are more inclined to want what their superiors or people they admire want. If, then, they derive some benefit from it, they will be grateful to you and they will say so, remembering that it came from you as if from a fountain (p. 378).

The study of humanities grants the government's authorities not only pleasant and satisfying personal benefits, but it also enhances their political acumen. Moreover, by acting as models of learning for the citizenry, those in the positions of authority can inflate their prestige.

Fluency in Latin was essential to the humanist endeavor: Interpretive skills provided the key to unlock the knowledge of the Ancients for the politician and citizen, as well as the scholar and religious; expressive skills granted the ability to communicate that knowledge to others. In a letter written to his renowned Venetian student, Leonardo Giustian, Guarino first compliments Leonardo on a Latin translation of Plutarch's *Cimon,* a translation that "seems not to be a translation, but produced by you as an original." Then he proceeds to thank his former student and others like him who, through their knowledge of Greek and Latin, ensure that "people who have been silent to us for so long, now, finally, have been restored to friendship with us [...] they live, and they converse intimately with us" (p. 316). The utility of scholars who could fashion translations of the Greek texts into Latin was keenly felt because fluent teachers of Greek were scarce, and Greek was virtually unknown even among scholars. Although fluency in both classical languages was the ideal, competence in Latin was deemed essential for everyone as translations of Greek texts became more available. The ability to interpret and express ideas in Latin was necessary for the realization of one's full potential as a human being.

In addition to interpretive skills and written expression, functional oral competence was fundamental to the *studia humanitatis* because Latin served as the language of wider communication for not only scholarship, but also for trade and government among the educated peoples of the continent. Guarino explains the importance of fluent speaking ability:

> To be admired for fluency, to be appreciated for speaking good Latin, is beginning to be true of the period, not just of individuals, so that today one is less likely to be praised for speaking well than to be criticized for speaking badly; today we are expected to speak good Latin, more so than in the past when we were criticized for speaking a barbarous language (p. 420).

Interpretive skills granted the student access to the knowledge contained in the ancient texts and expressive skills allowed the conveyance of new applications and ideas rooted in that knowledge to the wider community. Because it constituted a prerequisite for participation in the discourse of the world community, oral and written fluency in Latin was organic to the *studia humanitatis*. But how was that fluency to be attained in a period when Latin was no longer the mother tongue even in Latinic Italy?

---

*P*ause to consider . . .

the practical role that Latin held in the early study of humanities. It was an international language—the *lingua franca*—among scholars, world leaders, and business people for several centuries, and all important texts were written in Latin. What is the objective of second language instruction today? Is the realization of one's full potential as a human being still a viable goal? Does the study of foreign languages unlock the knowledge of other cultures?

GUARINO GUARINI AND BATTISTA: LIKE FATHER, LIKE SON?

Guarino appears in the annals of history because of his role in the establishment of the new curriculum of humanities, but all accounts laud his reputation as an outstandingly effective teacher of Latin and Greek. His pupils were among the most highly respected and well-known scholars of their day. Royal and influential families sought his services as a teacher of their children. However, even though a respected editor and translator of numerous ancient manuscripts, most notably those of Plutarch, Guarino authored no texts on his pedagogics, leaving behind only an epistolary legacy from which to discern his views on language learning and teaching. His letters are not the classical treatises of a preprinting press society. Those treatises were written in the form of a letter to an important person to ensure their preservation and distribution. Guarino's letters are, for the most part, short (two to three pages on average) notes to present and former pupils. They include personal references to family, health, and shared experiences, very similar to what we understand as correspondence. Without a teaching manual of his own authorship, Guarino's thoughts on education are transmitted in a document entitled *De ordine docendi et discendi,* [*The Program of Teaching and Learning*] written in 1459 by his son, Battista Guarini.

Although Guarino's son has not enjoyed the same historical prominence as Guarino himself, in his day Battista was considered an important figure in his own right. A student of his father's school, Battista was an admirable classicist, fluent in both Greek and Latin, a teacher, a respected philologist, and prolific translator. He was called to Ferrara upon the death of his father to take over the administration of Guarino's school. Despite his accomplishments, Battista is little mentioned in the histories of Western education, except for his pedagogical treatise which was always assumed to be a faithful rendition of his father's educational vision (Woodward 1921). In some instances, chroniclers blend the two figures, conflating father Guarino Guarini and son Battista Guarini, into "Guarino" as if the two were indistinguishable (Kelly 1969; Cole 1950). Boyd (1966) notes, however, that the father and son should not be confused, in that the father's decision not to write a pedagogical treatise and the son's attempt to do so signifies a relevant distinction in their perspectives on methodology.

Guarino and Battista differed in ways other than the type of texts that they authored. As we shall see from his writing, Guarino deserves his reputation as an outstanding teacher. That he was knowledgeable is without question. In addition, he was caring, affectionate with his students, and concerned that learning (and teaching) be pleasant. He saw the person as central in that experience, and his recommendations often revealed an intimate understanding of the learner's perspective. Above all, he viewed himself as a guide in the learning process. Conversely, Battista, while also a scholar, was clearly more of a director than a guide. Obsessed with order, rules, and procedures, he was so preoccupied with method that he seemed to forget why people learn languages, or even that people were involved at all! As a consequence, the son's treatise often does not accurately reflect his father's view of language teaching. The discrepancy between Guarino's beliefs about second language learning and Battista's manual for teaching illustrates the importance of maintaining theory when prescribing practice.

P*ause to consider* . . .

how likely it is that two people would view an event in exactly the same way. What might color their interpretations? Invite two people to observe one of your lessons and to record what they saw. How difficult is it to accurately convey both the action and the intent of another person's behavior?

Guarino's Letters and Battista's Treatise

Battista wrote his educational treatise, *De ordine docendi et discendi*, in the form of a letter to his student Maffeo Gambara da Brescia. He begins with the statement of purpose:

> I believe it is my duty as a teacher to propose for you a program-matic outline that will allow you to satisfy in the most efficient man-ner your avidity [for the liberal studies]. [...] Here you will learn the gradual order that teachers must follow in teaching and students [must follow] in learning Greek and Latin [...] a complete summary of the art of teaching and learning (in Garin, p. 434).

From the outset, Battista expresses his belief that teachers are constrained by their very profession to provide "programmatic outlines" that render "effi-cient" instruction. Moreover, he believes that teaching and learning proceed in a gradual, orderly fashion and that the discipline can be conveyed summarily.

In an effort to establish the authenticity of his document for his contem-poraries, Battista invokes the reputation of his father, maintaining the fol-lowing:

> I do not hesitate to claim that those who shall be taught with this method will find themselves numbered among the most educated of persons: In fact, I have united all those practices that (not only in my opinion—given my young age, my opinion wouldn't carry much weight—but according to the most learned men, above all my illus-trious father, granted, as you know, many years' teaching experience) seem most ideal for teaching on the one hand, and studying on the other. As you read, understand that it isn't I who speak, but my father, and rest assured that nothing that has been written is untried (pp. 434-436).

Accordingly, one would expect to discover in his treatise the secret to Guarino's success as a language teacher. However, a careful examination of Guarino's own letters reveals that, although some of what Battista writes in the *De ordine* faithfully echoes his father's words on language teaching, many extensions of those thoughts belie Guarino's original ideas and, in fact, imperil his vision.

Even on the surface, the father's and the son's texts differ in a number of ways. The authors' voices are distinct, and the tone and vocabulary of the letters and the treatise contrast starkly. Battista's text contains multiple references to "rules" and "norms," "order" and "method," "precepts" and "habits," "accuracy" and "correction," while Guarino's letters are filled with personal, fatherly advice and visionary metaphors. What follows is a juxtaposition of the two sources for their treatment of parallel topics: the purpose of second language study and the course that learning a second language takes, the contributions of reading and writing in that process, and the manner of error correction. The comparison of the father's letters and the son's treatise reveals how Battista fails to convey the humanist spirit that characterizes Guarino's views on language learning and teaching.

PURPOSE AND COURSE OF SECOND LANGUAGE STUDY

Both Guarino and Battista agree that Latin must be acquired as a living, practical language for it to be one that students can use to convey new ideas. Therefore, they argue that the first emphasis in instruction should be on meaning, rather than on form. This emphasis is consonant with the new curriculum's focus on the content of texts and the early reading of classical authors. But as we have already seen, the *studia humanitatis* were not limited to the development of interpretative skills. Here, too, father and son both affirm that oral fluency comes only when students acquire "the habit of speaking continually in Latin" (p. 442). Moreover, Guarino recognizes that this capacity comes gradually. He cautions the teacher, "don't expect from a baby's lips the learning appropriate to a mature adult" (p. 420) and he proffers the following advice on how to approach a difficult text:

> Don't be frightened if at first you don't understand; limit yourself to knocking on the door and calling again: the door will open and someone will answer (p. 345).

Guarino understands language learning to be a developmental process, one that progresses in stages. He cautions against harboring expectations that are not commensurate with the learner's stage of development. Moreover, he indicates that with experience competence will eventually emerge. Interestingly, even though Guarino wrote a grammar—*Regulae*, a derivation of Priscian's Latin grammar, in which he divorces grammar from dialectics, simplifies it, and redirects it to classical sources—he rarely mentions it. In fact, the study of rules as a prerequisite to language development is conspicuously absent from his advice. Instead, Guarino advocates immersing oneself in the original texts as the best way to acquire a language. His position on how language is learned through text will become clearer in the discussion of reading in the curriculum.

With regard to the primary importance of meaning in the interpretation of texts, Battista echoes his father's conviction when he writes "students begin by grasping the reasoning and the moral content [of the text], before they direct themselves to oratorical embellishments" (p. 465). But the exhortation that meaning take precedence over form, especially in the early stages of instruction, is diluted later by a lengthy section of the treatise entitled, *Fundamental Rules to Teach*. In this section, Battista expresses the belief that learning "certain fundamental rules" is an efficient method of assuring that students attain fluency. He states:

> I would like everyone to teach certain "fundamental rules" for the purpose of moving students quickly and surely to the aims of learning the rules (p. 442).

What are these basic rules? Battista provides several examples:

> They [students] should practice distinguishing active verbs from neuters according to the following: that neuters don't have the passive form in the first or the second person when the one who speaks is a person. One can't say "I was plowed" "You were plowed." Analogously, it helps to accustom students to observing the series of actives that, distributed in six classes, have in the first only the subject and the object; in the others, other than the object in the accusative case, they can have other cases, except the first, in successive order. The theory of passives is very brief: None of these requires anything except that the reciprocal conversion of the subject and of the object through the changing of the cases. What can be said of the much more compendious theory of the neuter? In fact they are in the same situation as the actives, and even the same constructions, except that they don't have the accusative. In fact those that are called transitive neuters, even though they have the accusative, nevertheless don't require, like the actives, two words in the same case. The deponents follow the same formula as the neuter. I have proposed only a few examples so that my thoughts [on the topic] will be clear (pp. 442-444).

If nothing else, the stifling style of the grammarian, the suffocating rhythm of an almost legalistic mind—so evident in this passage—attest to Battista's obsession with grammatical taxology and syntactical casuistry.

Despite his proclamation that his explanation is clear, it is hard to imagine how rules like those Battista has supplied might be helpful, let alone fundamental, in the acquisition of functional language competence. Battista, however, is convinced of the central importance of explicit instruction with regard to norms, and he states that while many books are available, he heartily recommends his father's, *Regulae*. In addition to advocating a prescriptive grammar, Battista warns that access to a reference grammar alone is not sufficient and that "teachers must pay attention to this: they must require students to apply these rules with written and oral exercises" (p. 442). He reminds teachers:

> Going over a rule only once isn't enough. You must go back to it two, three times, if necessary, until [the students] have it at their fingertips. And it's not a bad idea, even when they have gone on to more arduous studies, to return to the rules so that they never forget them, no matter how much time has passed (p. 446).

In Battista's theory of language teaching, rules are not only fundamental, or means to obtaining linguistic proficiency, they are an end in themselves. As he proceeds to outline the program of study in the treatise, he advises that, after the teaching of precepts, the instructor should move to the teaching of syllables and verses, and he expresses his admiration for the Ancients' attention to "minute details," such as syllabic feet, explaining:

> There are certain expressions with very different meanings that one can distinguish only on the basis of the length of a syllable. And, finally, even if they [syllable lengths] weren't good for anything, it would be worthwhile to study them just for the pure pleasure of it (p. 446).

It is clear that for Battista prescriptive norms and "minute details" of language are important, interesting, and even enjoyable topics of study. In taking this position, he reflects the medieval preoccupation with grammatical form and distances himself from both his father's pedagogy and the *studia humanitatis* with their focus on content through early exposure to texts and the development of functional language proficiency.

With regard to the pleasurable aspects of learning, as the quotations from his letters to persons in positions of authority imply, Guarino is adamant that the *studia humanitatis* be an enjoyable, as well as useful, enterprise for learners of any age. He claims "as you well know, how much these studies turn out to be pleasant for children, welcomed by adolescents, fruitful and fertile for more mature persons" (p. 321). However, the fact that such learning is pleasant for the individual does not imply that it carries no responsibility along with it. Just as Guarino insists that people in positions of authority act as models for the rest of society by encouraging the spread of the *studia humanitatis* through their own example, his certitude that people learn by example also pervades his beliefs about language teaching. He states:

> An essential pedagogical device, in teaching and in correcting, is to abstain from any impolite word, from any rude threat, from any obscene curse. Students, in fact, learn speech habits from their teachers, so that when they are reprimanded with curses and angry outbursts, in reality, they are encouraged to imitate [the same] (p. 344).

Guarino is thoroughly convinced of two axioms: (1) that students learn through exposure to good models; and (2) that the learning experience must be pleasant and practical. Moreover, he does not mention once in any of his letters the importance of learning rules of the type that Battista records. The combination of these facts leaves one very doubtful that Guarino would advocate the study of rules that serve no practical purpose or would agree that students find great satisfaction and utility in the study of syllable length.

Not only is Battista not persuaded that exposure to good models is sufficient for learning, he was firmly in favor of early and explicit instruction in surface-level linguistic features. Moreover, he advocates strict attention to accuracy from the beginning. In his recommended order of study he lists first pronunciation, then the declination of nouns and the conjugation of verbs, in preparation for the study of grammar. His use of absolute terms and restrictive adverbs, underlined in the passage, reflect his convictions as he warns:

> It is *important* to *accustom* students to pronounce *clearly* and *readily* letters and words, *not too fast, not too slowly*. Moreover, the teaching of grammar *must* be *perfect in every detail* because, just as buildings without *solid* foundation *collapse* when built upon, the same in studies: If students don't possess to *perfection* the elementary notions, the further one progresses the more apparent weaknesses become. Therefore, in the first place, children *must* learn to decline nouns and to conjugate verbs: Without this *there is no way* they will be able to grasp more complex notions (p. 440, emphasis mine).

Battista's own language underscores the intensity of his beliefs. In a similar way, in his reminder to teachers of their responsibility to monitor students' progress he predicates the necessity of reiteration in instruction:

> The teacher *must* not be content with having taught something once, but with *frequent repetitions over and over again*, he should exercise the children's memories, and like a scrupulous master, [the teacher] *must* know what they have learned and to what extent they have learned it" (p. 440, emphasis mine).

Battista places a heavy burden of responsibility on the teacher who is held accountable for what students know and how well they know it.

How different is his image of the teacher as a "scrupulous master" from the one presented by Guarino of "affectionate father" (pp. 310, 364) who continually addresses his students as "dearest" (pp. 306, 318, 334, 342, 346, 358, 360).

To recapitulate, Battista advocated the explicit teaching of rules, focused attention on discrete points of pronunciation and grammar, and maintained that accuracy, from the beginning, was fundamental to ultimate attainment in second language competence. Conversely, Guarino stresses the acquisition of competence in a second language as a gradual, developmental process; he views the teacher as a guide and model of competence that learners will use in that process. According to Guarino, interpretive skills come first, acquired through immersion in the language, exposure to excellent models, and access to interesting and useful texts. Fluency in oral and written expression develops gradually, as a consequence of exposure to good models and pleasant interaction in the second language. Based on these beliefs, is it possible to determine how Guarino's method of teaching may have looked? To answer that question, we must return to the change in the curriculum that the *studia humanitatis* represent.

THE ROLE OF READING IN LANGUAGE LEARNING

Because the new learning was based on the content of recently discovered classical texts, the fulcrum of the humanist curriculum rested on one's ability to read classical Latin and Greek authors. Guarino expresses his belief in the central importance of texts in a letter to Ludovico Gonzaga, son in the ruling family of Mantova. Ludovico is 12 years old and considered "advanced" in his studies, when Guarino writes:

> Do you desire outstanding advisors, the best, that is, in terms of faithfulness, beneficence, prudence? Then search out books. Read them. Make it a habit to carry them with you always, in the countryside and while traveling, as others do with dogs, falcons, and dice (p. 338).

In making his recommendation, Guarino once again stresses the practical benefit that is derived from reading. Books are a source of excellent advice for a future leader, and he associates text with all the trappings of a fifteenth century adolescent's entertainment: dogs, falcons, and dice. Guarino insists that reading must be a lifelong habit of everyone, not just students. In another letter, to Martino di Matteo Rizzon, a beloved pupil who himself became a teacher, Guarino admonishes "You should read, too—so that you continue to learn as well as teach" (p. 344). For Guarino, reading books is the ultimate experience. But his obsession with practicality is revealed when he points out that books are not only sources of wisdom and knowledge, but valuable in another way as well:

> I would prefer you have more books than clothes. Not only are books more useful and pleasant, they are also a good investment. You'll always be able to sell or exchange books, but one can't say the same for clothing (p. 344).

In contrast to his father's reverence for any text—unqualified!—Battista limits his treatment of books to the recommendation that, while they are not as important as a good teacher, "they should be correct and free from errors" (pp. 444-446). In fact, Battista's references to books are largely limited to a discussion of his discovery in several books of a faulty rule on comparative constructions which, according to his philological argument, was based on a corrupted letter in a manuscript (pp. 444-446).

If not through the study of grammatical and syllabic rules, however, then how are Guarino's students to acquire the literacy skills necessary to the reading of the ancient authors? In a letter to Lionello d'Este, Guarino offers "useful" advice on how to approach a text. In doing so, he suggests "some rules" and his most explicit description of "a kind of method:"

> In order to be useful to you in your studies, if not with my work at least with my advice, I will propose briefly, Prince Lionello, some rules, a kind of method, that I learned from Manuele Chrysoloras, my teacher of virtue and doctrine, while he was my guide on the path of letters. First of all, you must read, not whispering and mumbling the words, but pronouncing them with great clarity; a rule that, according to the medical profession, helps the digestion, and that succeeds as no small aid to understanding and perceiving better, since it's like having another talk to you, the ears stimulate the mind and encourage it to learn. Moreover, when the verbal construction and the meaning, the clause as some call it, the sentence as others call it, is clear, go over it again giving particular visual and mental attention to it, and if you grasped the meaning at the first reading, summarize and synthesize it in a single idea; if, instead, it escapes you and 'remains hidden to you' go back, knock so to speak on the door, until even if it takes time, it opens just a crack to your understanding. Here, you should imitate your hunting dogs that, if rummaging through bush and shrubs they don't find the bird on the first try, receive the order to repeat the procedure, because that which doesn't emerge at the first attempt might be flushed at the next (p. 380).

In stark contrast to Battista's absolute statements of pedagogy, even when Guarino used the term "rule," he immediately reduced it to possibility and suggestion. Notable also was his careful explanation of metalinguistic terms, "the verbal construction and the meaning, the clause as some call it, the sentence as others call it." Although his tone was soft-spoken, his intent was clear: When encountering a text, the reader should first attend to comprehension. Guarino states this explicitly, "when the verbal construction and the meaning [...] is clear" take note of it. He reminds the reader through two everyday images, knocking on the door and hunting, that detecting meaning in a text contains a similar element of surprise and discovery. The benefits to the digestion that reading aloud conferred was a long-held belief of the ancients; thus, in addition to all of its other advantages, reading is healthy!

Having completed the first step of the method, understanding the message, Guarino suggests how the reader may best retain what has just been read (in a pre-press age it should be remembered, when one might have to rely on borrowed texts):

> And when with the same care you have read the various phrases connected one to the other, before going on in the reading, use your knowledge and recapitulate to yourself what you've read. Don't go word by word, rather pay attention only to the meaning, and as though you were trying to grab a body not an appendage. If then, in the course of the reading, you happen to discover a nice saying, a wise and noble action, a quick answer, something pertinent to a gracious way of living, it seems to me that you would do well to learn that passage by heart; if you want to remember it really well, you need to repeat it more than once, [...] recalling to mind in the evening what you have learned during the day; and, once a month, you'll need to refresh your memory of all of the sayings.
>
> You'll also be able to remember many things better if you find someone with whom you can talk about them, and to whom you can share your thoughts; this in fact is the strength and nature of memory, not to remain inactive, but to improve day by day through exercise. On this note, one can give some useful and proven advice: When you have to read, keep at hand a little notebook like a faithful depository in which you might make notes of points in the text; in this way you will be able to go back to your favorite parts, without having to page through everything. [...] But if copying things in the notebook causes annoyance and interrupts your reading, you should find a capable, cultured young man, there are many around, to do this job and give it over to him (pp. 380-382).

In these two passages, we find Guarino's most explicit description of his "method" for language acquisition through reading. He recommended that the reader use multiple resources to assign meaning: phonological and visual cues, in addition to one's background knowledge. He advised the reader to stop and recall in one's own words what has been read. He acknowledged rereading as an effective strategy for ensuring comprehension, and he insisted that the reader not waste time decoding the text word for word, recommending instead that global meaning take precedence over word-level skills. Guarino was also careful to engage the reader in interaction with the text: to summarize and to synthesize the meaning, to take notes of personally interesting expressions, to jot down favorite passages, and to speak with someone else about the text's content. Finally, he admonished that the reader should do nothing that would sacrifice fluent reading or the text's coherence and cohesion. In Guarino's opinion, any rule or method that detracts from the pleasure of the quest for meaning should be avoided. Guarino's method of teaching reading was consistent with his general theory that language competence develops in stages from meaning-driven activity and exposure to good models (oral and written) in a supportive environment. How, then, are these beliefs and practices regarding the teaching of reading transmitted in Battista's pedagogical treatise?

One of the most obvious examples of Battista's misrepresentations of his father's pedagogy is found in his recommendations on how to approach a text, located in the section of the treatise entitled, *How to Study*. In each instance, Battista echoes and then reinterprets his father's advice to reflect his own beliefs about language learning. First, Battista reminds teachers that students shouldn't be allowed to rely only on the teachers' lectures; instead, they should read the original texts and the secondary sources that deal with the authors they are studying. After providing a list of recommended authors, Battista concedes as a matter-of-course the importance of meaning when he states that "above all, they [students] should get something out of what they read." However, with the immediate addition of the qualifying phrase "those things that are most worthwhile to remember and difficult to find," Battista eliminates the reader's personal response to the text that Guarino advocated in favor of a prescribed response (p. 460). Later, he counsels students: "when reading, don't stop before reaching the end of the sentence" (an echo of Guarino's suggestion to grasp the meaning of an entire clause), followed by "and if you don't understand at first, you will have to go back to the beginning and reread it two or three times more carefully, until the meaning becomes clear to he who diligently seeks it" (p. 464) (Battista's translation of Guarino's "knocking" and "hunting" metaphors). Finally, here is how the last piece of Guarino's counsel is rendered in Battista's work:

> First pay attention to this: Note the variety and the multiplicity of the vocabulary items. Don't just memorize them, but also write them down. Better yet if the annotations are written neatly and in an orderly fashion. These assiduous written exercises impress the words better upon the memory, and they highlight the accents of which that language [Greek] is full (p. 452).

In Battista's treatment of reading, one barely recognizes Guarino's recommendation of a "little notebook" in which to record where one's favorite passages occur. It has become, in Battista's interpretation, a vocabulary list and an exercise to learn "accents." Battista concludes the section with a recommendation to accompany reading with translation—as translation is "an exercise that gives one a wealth of vocabulary and a readiness of speech" (p. 452). In fact, he maintains that "many things that can fool the reader cannot escape the translator" (p. 452). For Battista, reading in a second language is an arduous decoding task. Filled with pitfalls for the unwary, it is mastered only through diligence, exactitude, and the memorization of vocabulary. Despite his attempts to convey the importance of meaning and to offer specific techniques, Battista's directives fail to transmit the essential theory underlying his father's approach to reading.

WRITING AND COMPOSITION

Important as reading is for the study of letters, the goal of instruction does not end there. The role of Latin in the study of humanities is to make students fully competent in all modes of communication, expressive as well as interpretive: They were expected to write, as well as to read and speak. In his comments on writing, Guarino remained consistent with his view that language is primarily a means of communication and that the *studia humanitatis* furnishes an eminently practical education. The study of the past was the most important subject in the new curriculum; however, no history books exist.; One of the responsibilities of the student trained in humanities is to transmit this information to others. In a letter to his student Tobia del Borgo, Guarino counseled the blossoming historian on how to write about history. He prefaced his advice with an explanation of the military's need of persons educated in the humanities. Only such persons will be competent to record heroic deeds for future generations. He claimed: "It is important to create writers who are able to record the [heroic] efforts and who can picture them in their writings, to avoid that the memory of the men should die with the men" (p. 384). But ever aware of the civic responsibility that a humanistic education carries, Guarino exhorts the writer to remember that texts serve different purposes. Because "there's a big difference between history and poetry" (p. 388), the historian must remain objective, distinguish between *historein* and *historîa* (the observable and the spectacle) (p. 386) and omit interjection of personal bias and opinion (p. 392). Guarino states:

> There is only one thing that I would prescribe as the most important above all: Don't get carried away by emotion, rather be free to write even that which isn't flattering. Don't refrain from telling the truth in order to further your ends. Don't glory in the destruction of the enemy (p. 390).

The truth is available to the writer, but it is not subservient to ulterior or personal motives. Just as political authorities have the moral obligation to use their education to act as models for the citizenry, so historians have the duty to record the truth, accurately and without bias.

As far as the actual composition task is concerned, Guarino first focuses his attention on the initial stages of the writing process: brainstorming, organization, and verification of the facts. Before anything else, he advises devoting time to thinking about the topic and jotting down ideas:

> First of all, you should collect all the events that you want to recount, summarily, in an unorganized heap, confused and unpolished as your brain offers them up, without stopping to ponder them, what one might call *aposchedîasma* [do it quickly, as it happens, without preparation]. And all this, with the parts still fuzzy and mixed up, should remain private: first in your head and later in your notes, like a sculptor who wants to carve a horse or a bull roughs out the figure before beginning to delineate the shoulders or the legs. [...] That pile under one's eye is very helpful to the mind, and according to need, can be like class notes. They follow, in spatial and chronological order, so that one can organize them and finally elaborate upon them (p. 386).

By now, Guarino's voice is readily identifiable by the reader; he speaks to the student as one who knows how messy the writing process is. His metaphor of the sculptor suggests a belief that composition is a craft, characterized by rough and incomplete aspects in the early stages, containing the promise of the finished product. Next, Guarino turns his attention to the organization of the writing:

> Once you've decided on the content of the exposition, first mentally and then in a summary, it will be easy for you to figure out which paths to follow and which to avoid. Some people, careless about the actual events, throw themselves into an eulogy of the princes or the condottieri, to the point that they waste time (p. 386).

In this section, Guarino proposes the preparation of an outline in order to structure the composition. Having such a plan makes the composition process easier and more efficient because the writer knows the purpose of writing and its course. Next, Guarino warns the writer to be accurate, to verify information, and not to rely exclusively or uncritically on secondary sources:

> It will make your exposition much clearer if, once in a while, you ask experts for information about strategies, troops, methods of foraging, etc. And if you need to mention these in your writing, don't be naive and rely solely on what you've heard. Remember what Flaccus said "The eye is a more reliable witness than the ear" (p. 388).

The reader of history has the right to expect that the information conveyed is accurate. Throughout his advice, Guarino reminds the writer to be considerate of the reader. In an earlier quote, he reprimands writers who do not remain focused and "waste time." In reference to specific features of text organization, Guarino proposes that the writer:

> Use introductions. These are useful for two reasons: They direct [the reader's] attention and develop trust, and you can use them to preface in an efficient way the fundamental points [of your argument] and their importance for future readers or listeners (p. 390).

The "implied reader" of modern theories of composition exists in Guarino's approach to writing. A text does not exist in isolation: It communicates to the reader; it is an interaction on paper.

In anticipation of the student's perennial query, "How long should it be?" Guarino states "whether the introduction is short or long will depend upon what follows" (p. 390). He reiterates that the length of the preface matters less than its function in relationship to the whole argument. He continues, "I think that the reader would be happy, if, at the very beginning of the treatise, especially if it's about war, you would lay out the causes of the events and the origins of the dispute" (p. 390), and he suggests that the writer "anticipate the reader's doubt" by using *prolepsis;* that is, by answering in advance possible questions the reader may have (p. 394). Even in terms of stylistics, the audience must be heeded:

> The style should be rich with expressions used by authoritative authors, open, virile, so that it renders the facts efficiently, not using foreign terms, not artificial, not obscure, not extraordinary, but clear, worthy, serious, so that everyone can understand, and so that educated people can admire and praise it (p. 392).

According to Guarino, no place for ornamentation or excess exists in composition. Expressive skill is demonstrated by a clear, concise style that renders the writing both easy to understand and pleasurable to read. Guarino's counsel reflects a theoretical congruence in his treatment of both reading and writing.

Throughout his treatment of composition, Guarino contended that the primary goal of writing is the communication of ideas. He stressed the importance of keeping in mind one's purpose for writing and the intended audience. In exactly the same way in which he advocated the manner in which a reader should approach a text (i.e., focus on meaning; use multiple clues, background knowledge, and the text's organization as aids to understanding; and interact with the text), identical directives appear in his advice to writers (i.e., focus on meaning; provide background knowledge and the significance of the work; organize the text coherently; and keep in mind the implied reader). How faithfully does the son represent his father's views on composition?

In a section entitled, *On Writing a "Theme" as Elegantly as Possible,* Battista includes none of the above advice regarding the responsibility of the writer, the writing process, text organization and structure, the use of primary versus secondary sources, or the intended audience. Instead, he begins the passage with a reference to his previous discussion of grammatical rules, and recommends:

> It will be very useful that in the application of these rules one become accustomed to careful composing, for example, closing the discourse with a verb, and preposing that which depends on it to that on which it depends. In this way, it will be easier to guide them [the students] to an elegant style (p. 444).

The totality of Battista's reference to writing consists of a list of rules for using comparatives and lamentations regarding the errors in texts caused by the linguistic ignorance of copyists. The remainder of the section is devoted to an explanation of the importance of knowing Greek in order to fully appreciate Latin vocabulary and morphosyntax, accompanied by directives for how Greek should be taught: "not in the disorganized way that Greeks teach it, but by following rules" (p. 451). Moreover, he counsels:

> In teaching, the fact that verb tenses are formed according to a general rule is of utmost importance; and be careful that the students have at their fingertips the verbs that in Greek are called "anomalous." To such an extent that (this is extremely useful in that language) in the blink of an eye they can distinguish a noun from a verb and the tenses of the verbs. They will soon arrive at the point where they can respond accurately to frequent interrogations by the teacher. Then, little by little, they will come in contact with the [ancient] authors, starting with the easiest prose writers because you don't want to wear them out by the profundity of the content at the expense of practicing the rules that they have learned. [The rules], first and foremost, are what we consider the most important thing of all (pp. 450-452).

Not only did Battista omit most of his father's directions for composition, he failed once again to convey the theory that supports them, just as he did in regard to reading. Because Guarino was consistent in his theory and approach to second language teaching as a system of communication based on the interpretation and expression of meaning, the ultimate test of instructional success is whether the students have acquired functional language ability. Battista instead was convinced that language acquisition occurs as a result of systematic instruction in rules and their application, and that the test of competence lies in the explicit knowledge of those rules. In the final comparison between the two, the attitudes of father and son conflicted once again in their responses to a mundane feature of language acquisition: learners' errors.

ERROR CORRECTION

Learning implies a provisional state of competence, and perhaps no topic has received more sustained attention throughout the history of second language teaching than the subject of errors and the appropriate pedagogical response to them. Both Guarino and Battista were classroom teachers, and it is natural that they, too, would address the topic.

Guarino conveys his attitude toward linguistic errors from two different perspectives: where he is the one who corrects and where he is instead corrected. In reply to a request from Bartolomeo da Montepulciano, the pontifical secretary, for a copy of a book that Guarino has purportedly written,

Guarino responds in the most vehemently passionate tone encountered in any of his letters:

> Another paragraph of your letter asks me if I would send you a copy of a work in which you've heard said that I express my opinion on the translations of our day and, worse yet, in which I have collected the errors made by translators. If this gives pleasure to some, let them do it. I certainly have no motivation to go about gathering other people's mistakes, if there indeed are any. I know that one couldn't ascribe to me a more awful blame: In fact, what could be more uncivil than delighting in another's embarrassment? What bigger proof could I offer of my envy than to harm the reputation of learned people? I would have to be malicious and mean. [...] I'm not the type to read others' writings to look for errors and criticize maliciously. I read in order to see myself in them, to learn, to correct myself, and amend myself, to eradicate with their help my own faults, not theirs, to improve myself in speech and act. [...] [Whoever has accused me of this] has no reason to say that I seek out others' errors. That would be the epitome of incivility, of malevolence, of maliciousness, to treat in such a way people whom I can only praise (pp. 312-314).

Clearly, Guarino found insulting the accusation that he had compiled a list of other scholars' errors. Furthermore, he repeated the obligation of learned persons to affirm and act as role models for others. But Guarino's disinterest in error correction was not limited to the distastefulness of acting as corrector of his peers, as an examination of his reaction to being corrected demonstrates. A former student who, having found some of Guarino's early writings in Latin, had commented on the mistakes and barbarisms in it, was sent the following reply in which Guarino explains once again the importance of input in language acquisition:

> It happened to us just like it does to those who today come from Germany to Italy to learn Latin; if they surround themselves with uncultured persons with poor pronunciation, they learn to speak with mistakes and with a roughness of speech that, instead of caressing the ears, wounds them. If, on the other hand, they spend time with people who have a natural fluency of speech and a sweet accent, their speech will be fine and their voice a swan (p. 418).

Having attributed his early mistakes to the lack of exposure to good models, he confides that upon the discovery of the original classical texts, he was able to improve his own language skills and chides:

> So, dear one, if you find mistakes in my earlier writings, you'll have to blame the corrupt use of that earlier period. You should smile affectionately at the infancy of your father and at his babbling, not ridicule it. [...] When you've reflected on this, you will no longer be amazed at how I used to write and you won't judge my former style so severely (p. 420).

Using himself as an example, Guarino proves that he does not ascribe to the notion that learners' errors might become fossilized; he is aware of his own second language development. He also made the point that errors do not merit either ridicule or harsh judgment, rather that they are a natural part of language learning. And, finally, because learning should be delightful, Guarino abhorred the most extreme form of error correction: the practice of beating students. Instead, drawing once again on the belief that students model their behavior on the teacher, he advises an atmosphere conducive to learning maintained through example and authority:

> Don't forget that you are their teacher, not their pal. But you should make them respect you by your virtuous example and by your authority, not by the severity of your beatings (p. 354).

Everyone makes mistakes: students, scholars, and even teachers themselves. They are a natural and forgivable aspect of learning. However, with enough exposure to good language models and patience, linguistic competence can continually improve. Guarino said no more on the subject of error correction.

It is probably not surprising to discover that Battista's insistence on rules culminates in the message that errors are to be avoided at all costs. This is to be accomplished through explicit and meticulous instruction, a "teaching of grammar [that] must be perfect in every detail" (p. 440). In a veiled reference to the importance of good language models, Battista attributes learners' errors to faulty teaching. He explains that "above all it is important that initially youths not be entrusted to uncultured and unprepared teachers," not because such teachers may have an adverse effect on the students' morals, but because they will teach incorrect forms, "something that is very difficult [to eradicate] because, as Horace said, 'a new container retains for a long time the odor of that which it first held'" (p. 438). Rather than view errors as a sign of a developing language competence that will eventually become more fluent, Battista sees them as obstacles that can only be removed through authoritative intervention: "It is therefore necessary to work very hard to remediate students' knowledge; and only with great effort and time, in a long, slow process can one cancel the first error" (p. 438). Accuracy from the beginning, according to Battista, is the most effective strategy for reducing the number of errors that learners commit.

Unlike his father who found the task of searching out errors "malicious" and "mean," Battista proposes that students should be trained to ferret out errors. He suggests that "every once in a while, the teacher should say a wrong form to test the students' knowledge. It will be an important sign of their progress if [the students] show themselves capable of pointing out other people's errors" (p. 440). Once again, Battista equates linguistic progress with the knowledge of rules, not with functional language use, and linguistic competence with the ability to meticulously identify imperfections. Even given his obsession with rules, Battista, like his father, advises against beating students:

> It is also necessary to be absolutely certain that children are not subject to brutal beatings, appropriate to slaves, whereby often a generous spirit is so offended that because of the beating hates letters before having even tried them. You might add that, fearing a beating, children don't do their assignments themselves, bringing instead work that has secretly been done by someone else; a true disaster, because everyone is grossly fooled: the teacher who makes unfounded judgments, the student who doesn't understand what, dishonestly, he says he has done himself. It is therefore better and more useful to proceed in a kindly manner (p. 440).

Battista uses the Greco-Roman argument that freemen should not be subjected to physical punishment, such is reserved for slaves. Moreover, he learned from classroom experience that students would lie to avoid being beaten, certainly not a behavior to be promoted or condoned. If Battista had stopped at this point, one may suspect that, at least in reference to corporal punishment, he and his father would be in full agreement. But Battista continues in a reformist stance that we now recognize as typical:

> It's even better [than beating], once in a while, to make them fear a beating, as if it's just about to occur, because if a student has no fear at all of being beaten, that confidence might place him in grave danger of negligence (p. 440).

Technically, then, Battista opposes physical punishment just as his father does. However, Battista's use of threat and scare tactics is diametrically opposed to the spirit of education expressed in Guarino's writing.

CONCLUSION

A comparison of Guarino's letters and Battista's pedagogical treatise on parallel topics—namely, the purpose of second language study, the course that learning a second language should take, the roles of reading and writing in that process, and treatment of errors—reveals a misconstruction of Guarino's beliefs (i.e., theory) in Battista's directives for teaching practice (i.e., method).

Notwithstanding all evidence to the contrary, Battista concludes the *De ordine docendi et discendi* with the following assurance:

> This is the program of teaching and the rules for studying that my own father (your grandfather in studies), as learned as he is good, used to teach students. As far as their excellence is concerned, you should be sufficiently convinced by the fact that from his school, like from the horse at Troy, have exited true princes of culture. In fact, the

majority of those who have been instructed in these studies [*studia humanitatis*] in this our Italy and in other parts of the world have sprung from this font (p. 470).

Battista is right in his proud assessment of his father's renown as a teacher and as a major proponent of educational reform: the successful innovation of the curriculum to include the study of humanities. However, the juxtaposition of his text with his father's letters casts serious doubt on the validity of his claim that "this is the program of teaching and the rules for studying that my own father [...] used to teach students." Nonetheless, Battista's treatise ends with the promise:

> Therefore, if you will hold to these norms with all your heart, as they say, you will extract a fruit that is not merely adequate, but superior to that which we could even hope for based solely on your talent and genius, of which we have a high opinion (p. 470).

In the histories of Western education, Guarino is cited as the illustrious teacher, and Battista appears only as the author of the pedagogical treatise. After the death of his father, Battista ran the school at Ferrara, but beyond this, neither he nor the school receives further mention. The innovation of the curriculum proposed by the humanists and by Guarino in particular remained and spread, but what of its language teaching theory? Already obfuscated in *The Program of Teaching and Learning,* the document that was intended to disclose a proved method of language teaching and ensure its continuity, Guarino's theory vanishes. Subsequent generations of teachers who read the treatise and followed its precepts would be adopting Battista's theory of language teaching, not that of his father's. In doing so, they would work under the assumption that second language learning proceeds systematically through explicit instruction in grammatical rules, that accuracy from the beginning is necessary in order to avoid fossilization of errors, that reading in a second language is fundamentally an exercise in decoding, and that writing consists of the application of grammatical rules. In the pedagogical treatise, teachers would not encounter a theory that views second language learning as a gradual, developmental process. They would not understand why exposure to oral and written texts (discourse) in the second language is essential to that process. They also would have no inkling that a focus on interesting subject matter, early and sustained interaction with authentic texts, the interpretation and expression of meaning, and tolerance for errors provides the ideal environment for successful language acquisition.

Throughout this chapter we have seen that enough of Guarino's advice is misconstrued as to cast serious doubt that Battista's treatise on education is a true representation of the method of his father, notwithstanding his pledge and constant reassurances. The recommendations proposed by Battista serve to obscure rather than to mirror the spirit of teaching for which his father was extolled, because the theory which underlies Battista's recommendations is not congruent with Guarino's.

Regardless of whether Guarino and Battista differed in their actual classroom practice, what is vitally important in this explication is that Guarino's theory of second language teaching was not transmitted in Battista's treatise. Because of it, the beliefs about second language learning held by one of the most outstanding educators in language teaching history have remained virtually unknown, while the rigidly prescriptive methodology of his son has endured. The resultant lacuna in our historical perspective has allowed the persistence of a warped notion of what constitutes "traditional" language teaching.

Does any attempt to institutionalize a vision into a rigid methodology destroy the vision? Perhaps. In the history of second language teaching, distortion of theory as it is converted into method and conveyed to language teachers is certainly not peculiar to the case of Guarino and Battista. As we shall see in the next two chapters, it appears to form part of our language teaching tradition as well. In fact, the relationship between the theory and its interpretation in pedagogical manuals reflects the same pattern of incongruence each time. Yet, despite Battista's failure to convey it to classroom teachers, Guarino's theory of language learning and teaching resurfaces, time and again, in our historical journey. Interestingly, it never seems to be conveyed in the handbooks. The paradox will become more evident as we turn to educators from the centuries that immediately followed Guarino da Verona: Ignatius of Loyola (1491-1556) and Johannes Amos Comenius (1592-1670).

---

*P**ause to consider . . .*

that like Guarino, many outstanding teachers throughout the history of education chose not to write a "how to" manual. We can only surmise why this is so. Is it possible that they were so busy teaching that they didn't have time to write? Or that they found fulfillment in the act of teaching, rather than in its analysis? Who writes the language teaching manuals of today? What might the profession be missing by not excavating the unmined resource of excellent teachers in the field?

CHAPTER TWO

The Administrator: Implementation of the Curriculum

Ignatius Loyola (1491–1556)

In the study of humane letters and the languages there cannot be a set period of time for their completion, because of the difference in abilities and learning of those who hear the lectures, and because of other reasons, too.

—Ignatius Loyola,
Constitutions, Part IV, Chapter 15, 1551

There should not be more than five grades of lower studies [...]: one of rhetoric, a second of humanities, and three of grammar. [...] That this distinction [between grades] may be better and more easily preserved, all rules of Emmanuel must be divided into three books, of which each is appropriate to a single class.

—Ratio Studiorum of 1599

Today we are intimately immersed in information, swaddled by virtual, visual, and printed text. The Internet, satellite television, and personal computers bring people, places, events, and ideas from around the globe instantly into our homes, offices, and classrooms. How does a society react to all that information? Who has the authority to control it? Should all texts be readily accessible to everyone? Although innovations in text technology permit information to flow more quickly and easily, advances are seldom met with indiscriminately open arms. Each new technological pathway causes us to reconsider our relationship with the information that it brings.

At the end of the fifteenth century, Europeans witnessed just such a phenomenon, and society faced the same questions. A new technology had burst upon the scene. Because of it, information poured into courts, schools, and homes as never before: relentless and unstoppable. No longer would letters need to be painstakingly copied by hand to be shared. Books could be produced in a fraction of the time and at a greatly reduced cost, making them widely available. The Western world experienced its first taste of mass media: the printing press. It was original and so powerful that the intellectuals panicked. Who would control the flow of information? How could society be prepared to manage it? What kinds of skills would young people need to use it to their advantage? Literacy skills, of course. Where could they acquire them? In schools. But how, and in which language?

THE CHANGING ROLE OF LATIN

Until this time, Latin held sway as the language of scholarship of society's educated elite. Official documents, scientific manuals, and, of course, the works of classical authors were in Latin. Fluent expressive ability in Latin enhanced career opportunities, especially in government and diplomacy. However, despite the humanists' attempts to establish Latin as the language of wider communication among all the citizenry, the vernacular languages of Europe expanded in use and power. As the European nations of the sixteenth century began to forge identities along political, religious, and cultural boundaries, the emergent status of the vernacular languages fostered linguistic and patriotic alliances. Whereas everyone could communicate in the vernacular languages, only the privileged could use Latin.

The allegiance of fatherland and mother tongue would grow increasingly strong as cultural identities were carved out upon the European continent. If Latin *had* become the language of wider communication, then it might have served to unify the peoples of Europe, just as it did during the Roman Empire. Instead, one by one, nations experienced their glory years, first Italy, then Spain, the Netherlands, and France. Culture, no longer under the jurisdiction of the hierarchical Church, became the property of the state; it was in the best interest of a state that wished to assert its sovereignty to characterize itself through its unique cultural heritage. Vernacular languages and literatures formed part of that tradition. Thus, proponents of Latin as a second language were at odds with the move to nationalize.

The transition from Latin to the vernacular as the appropriate language for formal written communication did not take place without debate. In Italy, where the early humanistic voice was strongest, the resolution of the "questione della lingua" [the language question] resulted in the adoption of the dialect of Florence and Rome as the national literary language. The selection of that particular dialect reflected a fortuitous coincidence of linguistic history, cultural heritage, and political acumen. Florentine was the language variety most similar to Latin, thus its literature was comprehensible to those who could read Latin. Moreover, at the time of its adoption, it was the language of the peninsula's most influential group of bankers and financiers. Likewise in Spain, France, England, and Germany, vernacular languages gained acceptance as much for their political and economic clout as for their literary traditions.

At the same time, Spain was enjoying its peak of political and cultural influence. It introduced to the continent a variety of exotica from the New World: pineapples, coffee, and chocolate. Its explorers returned with tales of adventure and possibility. The enthusiasm for the discovery of the past, which had characterized the previous century, was overshadowed by the prospects for future glory: commercial, political, and cultural.

The explosion of changes experienced by European society disturbed the status quo to such an extent that it created a crisis. Efforts to manage the disruption, to provide stability, can be seen in the proliferation of attempts to regularize every aspect of life, from manuals of etiquette to the Protestant Reformation and Counter Reformation. Language use was not exempt from such orthodoxy. In 1547, French, not Latin, was declared the official language of the French authorities. The Accademia della Crusca, the first of the language academies, was established in Florence in 1582. Dedicated to the provision of guidelines for linguistic practices, this academy not only canonized Florentine as the cultural language of the Italian peninsula, it also sought to control the language's linguistic evolution. In this way, the cultural heritage of Italy's two preceding centuries would be defended and preserved. Similar academies with like purposes would arise in France and Spain during the next century.

The early humanists who had desired to bring about a rebirth of classical culture through the reinstatement of Latin were thwarted in their attempt to establish it as the international language for all European citizens. With the rise of national cultures, national languages served to characterize national identities. Moreover, the economic reality began to breed a new social entity: a class of merchants and bankers. The vernacular languages of the continent represented this nascent bourgeoisie. The middle class hankered after the trappings of the cultural elite and sought to have their children educated so that they too would have access to the benefits of the new technology.

Gradually, however, parents needed to be convinced of the utility of having their children learn Latin. Although it was still in considerable measure the language of scholarship, Latin was not the language of home, community, or commerce. Moreover, Latin was strongly associated with the Catholic Church, itself in a tumultuous position as a result of the political and theological attacks of the Reformation. The translation of the Bible into the vernacular, made increasingly available to the public by the rapid development of book printing, effectively eliminated the single most compelling motivation for literacy in Latin among the members of the newly formed Protestant sects: personal salvation.

Against the backdrop of a sixteenth-century Europe coping with every sort of novelty, the seeds of Latin's demise began to germinate. It was changing from the *lingua franca* of scholars to a prestigious, but foreign, language for the bourgeoisie. Despite the decline of wider pragmatic functions, the cachet associated with the ability to read and write Latin would persist for at least the next two centuries. The tension, however, between the practical concerns of a vernacular society and the status of the intellectual elite was reflected in the second language teaching methodology of the Jesuit school.

IGNATIUS LOYOLA AND THE *STUDIA HUMANITATIS*

Had it not been for a war injury that forced Ignatius Loyola to spend over a year in his sick bed recovering, the Societas Iesu [the Jesuit Order], might never have been founded. It is said that it was during his period of convalescence that Ignatius read an account of the life of Christ and *The Lives of the Saints* and was inspired to devote his own life to religious service (Fitzpatrick 1933). In his quest to promote religious devotion and to encourage others to act "for the greater glory of God," Ignatius fashioned a system of education that would garner the respect, if not always the approval, of generations. While his conversion story makes for fascinating reading, what is particularly interesting in the present context is Ignatius's academic preparation for such a task, particularly with regard to learning Latin.

Unlike Guarino Guarini and other humanists, Ignatius was not a lifelong scholar. Born to nobility the year before Columbus sailed on his first voyage from Spain, Ignatius spent his adolescence and young adulthood in military service and at court. It wasn't until after his spiritual conversion at age 33 that he began his formal education which was to last 11 years. By his own confession, he failed miserably in his earliest attempts to learn Latin, first with a tutor and then in a local school. Next, he studied grammar for one year at the University of Paris in the College of Montaigu which still taught under the medieval system. When Ignatius finally began the study of philosophy at the University of Paris in the College of Sainte Barbe, it was within a program in which "the teachers taught the ancient languages by the methods of the most advanced humanists of Germany and Italy" (Ganss 1954, p. 13). The humanist emphasis on the use of classical texts as the basis for interactive language use, which Ignatius ultimately experienced in Paris, profoundly influenced his own beliefs about language teaching. However, while his hard won preparation in Latin allowed him to complete his university studies in philosophy, Ignatius never acquired the ready fluency that was common among the Italian humanists or even many of his contemporaries. He composed much of his work in his native language, Spanish, relying on secretaries and colleagues for translations into Latin.

Cognizant of the role that competence in Latin (or lack thereof) played throughout his own education, Ignatius was thoroughly convinced that Guarino's *studia humanitatis* provided the necessary foundation for all other studies. Like Guarino, Ignatius argued his position from a quintessentially pragmatic perspective: The *studia humanitatis* were seen as the most practical means for the formation of any educated, moral citizen—government official, banker, or priest. Certainly, such a curriculum was important for the insight that could be gained from reading the classical authors. Even more compelling, it was also the method by which to acquire the language itself and, for Ignatius, the prestige that fluency in Latin conferred. Prestige and authority were central to the educational aims of the Society: namely, to marry the study of humane letters with Christian doctrine. The Church of the Counter Reformation would seek in the Jesuit schools the intellectual force of a humanist education combined with strict allegiance to Christianity.

Ignatius's contribution to the history of Western education was not an innovation in the content of the curriculum: He adopted essentially the curriculum already established by Guarino. The emphasis on religious education was not new either: The early humanists were fundamentally Christian in their pedagogy. Rather, Ignatius sought to regularize the study of humanities and to establish guidelines for teaching practice. His genius lay in the development of a detailed plan for the organization and implementation of the study of humanities. The codification of the instruction in the *studia humanitatis* would serve to cast the net of influence resulting from such an education across a wider public. In terms of systematization and control, Ignatius was as much a product of his time as the writers of manuals on courtly manners. His legacy was a blueprint for the wide-scale implementation of Guarino's innovation. When Ignatius died in 1556, he left an educational model whose structural features are still present in Western systems of education.

The Jesuit College System

Prior to the sixteenth century, formal education existed at two distinct levels: elementary and university. The elementary level imparted rudimentary skills in reading and writing, perhaps limited to knowing the ABCs and how to write them, and counting. For those who wished to pursue a formal course of education beyond the elementary level, a tutor or a local school run by the commune provided continuing instruction. Having acquired basic literacy, a student who had access to texts could read and study independently. Anyone with sufficient literacy skills in Latin to follow the lessons was eligible to enter the university, even at an age as young as 12.

As texts became more widely available and as more advanced literacy skills were required at all echelons in society, an intermediary level of instruction became necessary. The *colegio* [college], in Ignatius's Spanish, or in today's terms the "secondary school," was born of this need. Herein lay Ignatius's vision. He sought to establish a system of education that would make the study of humanities uniform for any young person desirous of learning. The only entrance requirements for the school were a familiarity with the alphabet ("how to read and write" meant how to form letters and read them) and the parents' permission:

> When this school has been advertised, all who desire are admitted to it free and without the acceptance of money or any present—that is, all who know how to read and write and who are to begin grammar, and who, since they are little boys, have the approval of their parents or guardians (*Letter to Father Antonio Araoz*, 1551, in Ganss 1954, p. 26).

The "little boys" (*niños*) for whom the college was intended ranged in age from 7 to 17, the majority 10 to 14 years old. Elementary education was not part of the plan due to lack of personnel and resources; instead, Ignatius was concerned with providing quality middle grade instruction. He advocated small, interactive classes to allow individualized attention. Professors were to tailor their lessons to students' levels of ability; the entire setting would be conducive to learning. Even among religious novices, no mortification of the flesh was allowed: no "fasts, disciplines, or chains" (*Letter to Father Urban Fernandes* 1551, in Young 1959, p. 235). Students were expected to be students, not flagellants. They were also understood to be boys; therefore, time was prescribed in the curriculum for daily recreation and weekly vacation. Correction was limited to instances of moral disobedience, and it was never to be administered by a teacher. The most severe punishment was dismissal from the college.

The instructional objective of the Ignatius system was that students exit the program equally articulate in three areas: the Latin language, the classical authors, and Christian doctrine. The *studia humanitatis* formed the core curriculum for all students, not just future Jesuits ("scholastics"), but for lay students ("externs") as well:

We take into account the plan that in our colleges not only our own scholastics are to receive their training in letters, but externs as well are to receive it both in letters and good morals. [...] Our intention would be that humane letters, languages, and Christian doctrine would commonly be taught in the colleges (*Constitution*, Part IV, Chapter 7, in Ganss, p. 308).

Although he does not include primary education in his plan, Ignatius is adamant that the fundamental mission of his educational system is to provide a general, secondary level of instruction. Attempts to give preference to more advanced subjects are strongly discouraged:

When there is a good number of students already grounded in humane letters, someone is appointed to inaugurate the course in the arts [logic, physics, metaphysics, moral philosophy, mathematics, natural science]. When there is a number of students well grounded in the arts too, someone is appointed to give the lectures of the course in theology, still according to the method of Paris, with much practice. Afterwards, this entire arrangement is continued. For, experience shows that it is inadvisable to begin by lecturing on the arts or on theology, since the students make no progress because of their lack of a foundation (*Letter to Father Antonio Araoz*, 1551, in Ganss, p. 27).

First and foremost, students are to learn language and content from the classical authors. The *studia humanitatis* provide the training that is relevant for all students, regardless of their station or career goals. Only after they have completed these studies should the program expand to include courses in logic and science. Ever the realist, Ignatius acknowledges that not everyone needs or wants to go beyond this middle level of instruction:

This [the caveats regarding higher levels of instruction] is understood to be about places where there is an inclination toward something more than humane letters, since that inclination does not exist everywhere. In those others it is sufficient to teach the languages pertaining to humane letters (*Letter to Father Antonio Araoz*, 1551, in Ganss p. 27).

Clearly, the fundamental educational mission of the society was to provide second language competence in Latin. The benefits of such a system were immediate:

They [the students] are occupied to a sufficient extent with their lessons. Much care is taken that all learn through lectures, disputations, and compositions. Thus provision is made for them to reap great fruit of letters (*Letter to Father Antonio Araoz*, 1551, in Ganss, p. 30).

These benefits were also long-lasting:

> From among those who are at present merely students, in time some will depart to play diverse roles—one to preach and carry on the care of souls, another to the government of the land and the administration of justice, and others to other occupations. Finally, since young boys become grown men, their good education in life and doctrine will be beneficial to many others, with the fruit expanding more widely every day (*Letter to Father Antonio Araoz*, 1551, in Ganss pp. 28-29).

The Jesuit college system appealed to parents who wished to have their children prepared to meet the demands of an increasingly literate workplace. It offered the best training for the future priest, government official, or merchant. It also kept young boys and adolescents out of trouble by keeping them gainfully occupied during the day. Whereas parents of previous generations might have entrusted their children's education to a particular scholar-tutor, like Guarino, confident that he would provide the appropriate course of study, they now needed to be persuaded by the benefits of an educational system, rather than by the reputation of an individual. What kind of academic preparation was necessary for the student who planned to attend the university to study mathematics or philosophy? What training would benefit the young person who intended instead to return to the family business after college? Parents were not certain what the content of the college curriculum should look like. It was a skepticism shared by some educators as well.

Why Study Humanities?

The Inseparability of Language and Content

The rationale for the *studia humanitatis* as the basis of the Jesuit college curriculum appears in a letter written by Ignatius's secretary, Polanco, to Father James Lainez in 1547. In an earlier letter, Father Lainez had expressed doubt that the humanities provided a suitable academic foundation because they were not a "rigorous" program of study. He feared that students would become soft if allowed to dally in such intellectual pablum. Consequently, they would find themselves unprepared to confront the challenges of more profound studies like theology and philosophy. Father Lainez had claimed that "excessive devotion to classical studies usually makes the mind so dainty and refined that it neither can nor cares to give itself to profounder studies" (*Letter to Father James Lainez*, 1547, Young, p. 133). To this charge, Polanco replies that moderation is the key even in literary studies, but that languages, in particular, require sufficient time and attention to be learned well:

I agree with your reverence on the point of excess in these studies, both because of the authority with which you write and because of the examples we have of those who, having begun higher courses, wore themselves out before they had worked very hard. [...] But notwithstanding the difficulty I see in tarrying too long in these studies, I should not think that it would be too long, speaking again in general, to remain long enough to master the humanities, especially languages (*Letter to Father James Lainez*, 1547, in Young, p. 133).

Language learning requires time; it is not something that can be accomplished hurriedly, in a rush to move on to more high-brow subjects.

Later in the same letter, Polanco reiterates that the time allotted to the study of Latin is well spent. What may seem to the naive observer an inordinate amount of time devoted to the acquisition of Latin he likens to a wise investment. He warns that failure to make such an investment turns language learning into a Sisyphian task: Those who fail to remain at their language studies until they reach a functional threshold of competence must continually start from the beginning. As evidence for his argument, Polanco cites his own unsuccessful attempts to learn Greek and Hebrew, and he concludes, "no one can get this mastery [of a language] who does not devote sufficient time and effort to it" (*Letter to Father James Lainez*, 1547, in Young, p. 136).

Throughout, it appears that Polanco concedes the developmental nature of second language acquisition and the length of time that is required for one to become truly proficient in a language. He also makes clear what he means by "master the humanities." In reference to a particularly promising student, Polanco explains why Ignatius wants him to stay "a little longer at these studies [the humanities]:"

It will do him no harm to know more Latin, although he is well advanced. He should see more of the authors, exercise himself in writing, and, as I said, master the language. Second, there will be plenty for him to learn in rhetoric and history (*Letter to Father James Lainez*, 1547, in Young, p. 136).

To "master the humanities" a student needs to read extensively and to gain fluent written competence. Exposure to additional texts will supply the interesting subject matter which will, consequently, hone interpretive and expressive skills.

One must keep in mind, however, that objections to the *studia humanitatis*, such as those raised by Father Lainez, would have an effect on the realization of the Jesuit college curriculum. In the final official document of the

Jesuit plan, a period of three years is considered sufficient to study Latin, and students are encouraged to spend less time than that, when possible. Apparently not only parents but also other Jesuits could not be convinced that a greater amount of time spent learning Latin was justified.

Throughout the remainder of the letter, Polanco enumerates several reasons why students should be versed in Latin, citing first "the authority of those who advise this study of languages as very necessary for Scripture." By whose authority was such study advised? It included not only Guarino and earlier generations, but also Ignatius himself. Polanco assures, "I say authority, ancient as well as modern; and I must admit that what has weight with me is to see that on this point Master Ignatius feels as I do, for he is very desirous of having members of the Society excel in Latin." Just in case his reader remains unconvinced by the advice of mere mortals, Polanco suggests that it is an authority that emanates from the Divine, "Over and above the human prudence and experience in which he [Ignatius] excels, I believe that God especially inspires him with such ideas and convictions" (*Letter to Father James Lainez*, 1547, in Young, p. 133). Despite the recent availability of vernacular translations of Scripture, the *studia humanitatis* were deemed essential to an informed understanding of biblical literature and its exegesis (Scaglione 1986). Especially during this period of religious unrest, the ability to defend one's convictions may become a lifesaving skill.

In addition to the argument that a higher authority demands the study of Latin, Polanco proposes that a knowledge of languages grants authority in and of itself. Competence in a second language bestows power upon an individual because "as everyone wants to have a knowledge of languages, it would seem that one who did not know them would exercise but little authority." With power comes influence, and competence in Latin, in addition to the mother tongue, allows the possibility to influence people outside one's own linguistic community, whether by preaching, in conversation, or through one's writing. Second language competence grants the power and authority to address a variety of audiences, including those that carry political or cultural clout. Polanco recognizes in the fluent use of Latin a realm of influence that "seems to be especially necessary in our Society" (*Letter to Father James Lainez*, 1547, in Young, p. 136).

How were 10 to 16 year olds to acquire the expertise in Latin that would serve them in their careers? The *studia humanitatis* provide the fundamental means to develop the second language skills which will, in turn, bestow influence and prestige upon the learner. Interestingly, these studies are useful not only for the end result that they produce, but also for the very process of learning. As subject matter, they motivate students. Polanco maintains that the humanities are an appropriate content area precisely because they are easier and more interesting for young people than are philosophy and theology. To allay Lainez's fear that students will suffer intellectual harm from such enjoyable studies, Polanco argues that they have a dilatant effect on the mind, opening it and readying it for more challenging work later on. Because of this, the humanities are, in fact, the most appropriate subject matter for the untutored because they are "better adapted to minds that have not yet been trained and are less robust" (*Letter to Father James Lainez*, 1547, in Young, p. 136). After all, Polanco argues that no less than the church fathers themselves, "the ancients, such as Jerome and Augustine and others of the Greek and Latin fathers," along with great thinkers of the past, "the Platos and Aristotles, for example, and other philosophers" provide proof that "the study of the classics in no way blunted the fine point of their minds to prevent them from penetrating into the heart of things" (*Letter to Father James Lainez*, 1547, in Young, p. 133).

Notwithstanding the pleasure and ease with which languages and letters are pursued, Polanco assures that "even in these studies there will be opportunity to exercise talent and intellectual muscle, especially when a student takes part not only in rhetorical disputes, if he is engaged in that study, but by means of original compositions, either in verse or prose, speeches, or letters" (*Letter to Father James Lainez*, in Young, p. 136). That Ignatius himself shares the opinion that intellectual activity accompany language study is apparent in his recommendations for frequent discussion and practice in original composition.

If divine and ecclesiastical authority, the prestige that second language competence endows, and the intrinsic quality of the *studia humanitatis* to motivate learning and prepare students for more profound subjects fail to convince the reader of the pivotal role that the humanities should play in the curriculum, Polanco resorts the power of tradition. He reminds his reader that such studies distinguish the erudite citizen from the barbarian:

> It seems that from times long ago right up to our own it has been a common practice to begin with classical literature, with the exception of those years when barbarism not only in literature but in society reigned in the place of study. With the exception of these years we gather that this method of beginning with a good foundation in literature before going on to other studies prevailed in Greece and Italy, and I think other places as well (*Letter to Father James Lainez*, 1547, in Young, p. 134).

Literature (i.e., reading) and Latin were intertwined. In reference to text and language, one was inconceivable without the other. How else would one learn Latin, if not through the classical authors? Why else would one want to learn Latin, if not to acquire the authors' wisdom? The dual purpose of attaining language and content area competence was the essence of the humanist curriculum.

Within this framework, "grammar"—as we call the rules that govern language use—was acquired through the study of history, composition, mathematics, science, poetry, and rhetoric. As Scaglione (1986) points out in his book, *The Liberal Arts and the Jesuit College System*, the difference between medieval education and humanism was not in the amount of time that was appointed to the study of "grammar," but rather in how that time was spent. He explains that:

> In the actual apportionment of time it might seem that an excessive amount of it was allocated to grammar, which in the elementary stages of instruction could officially take as much as most of the first four years. This had certainly been the case in the Middle Ages, where bulky and complicated manuals had to be painstakingly studied, minutely glossed, and thoroughly memorized. The humanists made valiant efforts to reverse this situation and reduce the study of rules to a minimum, assuming the inductive method to be the best and the soundest: The rules for both correctness and elegance, that is, grammar and rhetoric, could best be learned by direct exposure to the good literary texts, after only a modicum of introductory, schematic paradigms (Scaglione, p. 10).

The key to language acquisition was the study of texts, not rules; and the "good literary texts" were in Latin.

The classical authors were the mainstay of the humanist curriculum. From them, students would learn both the wisdom of the past and the language. Because language and subject matter knowledge were equally important goals in the curriculum, vernacular translations were not acceptable substitutes for the original texts. As long as language and content remained indissolubly linked, this situation would not change. Only when the two were separated would the vernacular translations become widely used. As a result, the instructional outcome would no longer entail the development of communicative competence in Latin.

Finally, because the ultimate goal of the Jesuit education was to use it to benefit one's neighbor, not simply oneself, Polanco admonished that only those who received an education that depended upon firsthand knowledge of the sources they were studying would acquire the depth of understanding required to share that knowledge with others. Reading commentary was not sufficient. Access to primary sources was essential. Furthermore, only students who interacted with text, interpreted it and conveyed its meaning orally or in writing, would be capable of expressing that knowledge to others. In this way, students educated according to Ignatius's plan would achieve "a more widespread good than they [the scholastic doctors] now do with all their learning" (*Letter to Father James Lainez*, 1547, in Young, p. 134). In other words, the Jesuit program sought to produce students who were able to put their language and literacy skills to use for the common good.

The *studia humanitatis* offered the surest means to educating young people to meet the demands of the sixteenth century. The Jesuit college provided the assurance that such instruction would be free, age appropriate, developmentally sequenced, morally sound, and supervised. The experience, in turn, would produce bilingual gentlemen who, by their example and influence, would bring others to Christ. It would also give them a competitive edge in their careers by the prestige and authority that a knowledge of Latin granted.

*P**ause to consider . . .*

that in the justification of an innovative curriculum, Guarino and Ignatius cite classical authors like Horace, Cicero, and Plutarch, as well as religious figures like the church fathers and Scripture to supply authority to their argument. As modern readers, teachers, and scholars, we may find such references unusual. Who are the "authorities" cited in the field of applied linguistics today? How are they selected?

IN HIS OWN WORDS: IGNATIUS'S VISION AS OUTLINED IN HIS LETTERS AND THE CONSTITUTIONS

Like Guarino, Ignatius believed that functional language ability would be acquired only through exposure to interesting texts accompanied by meaningful interaction in the language. However, in contrast to Guarino, who functioned as both administrator and principal teacher in his own school, Ignatius espoused a more ambitious and far-reaching plan: He sought to establish Jesuit colleges throughout all of Europe. Because his plan involved multiple teachers across various sites, the implementation of his system of education posed an administrative problem. How could Ignatius ensure that instruction would be uniform in colleges with diverse faculty and student populations in disperse locations? Clearly, some kind of document was required, one in which the instructional plan and its justification were delineated, so that administrators and teachers would know what was expected of them, how to conduct their schools, and why.

Every religious order has its own set of guidelines. The governing principles of the Society of Jesus are established in the *Constitutions*. Written between 1547 and 1550, then revised, Ignatius continued working on the *Constitutions* until his death. The ten sections of the document cover every aspect of Jesuit life, including the educational function of the Society. Ignatius deals specifically with his proposed system of education in the Fourth Part of the *Constitutions*. This section consists of seventeen chapters, and it constitutes half of the entire document. In addition to writing the *Constitutions*, Ignatius conducted a great deal of correspondence. Many of the letters are concerned with spiritual advice and fundraising efforts for the Society's work; but some of them, especially those written prior to the completion of the Fourth Part of the *Constitutions*, refer to matters of instruction and curriculum. Often Ignatius writes in reply to questions and concerns from fellow Jesuits who are attempting to implement his plan at various sites.

In both the *Constitutions* and his epistolary, what distinguishes Ignatius's writing from the work of his successors is the extensive amount of justification that Ignatius supplies to explain his every proposition. Polanco's letter described in the previous section, although written in the secretary's hand, is a good example of Ignatius's tendency to establish his position through copious explanation. As an administrator, Ignatius relies on persuasion rather than on dogmatism to further his pedagogical vision.

Instruction in Ignatius's system remains grounded in the study of Latin and humane letters. The insistence on the development of learners' functional ability in Latin is paramount: "The order to be observed in the subjects is that a solid foundation should be laid in the Latin language before the liberal arts" (*Constitutions*, Part IV, Chapter 5, in Fitzpatrick 1933, p. 73) so that "all be well grounded in grammar and the humanities" (*Letter to Father Urban Fernandes*, 1551, in Young, p. 236). As to how this solid foundation should be acquired, Ignatius advocates that students acquire interpretive skills through their attendance at the daily lectures. These lectures are conducted in Latin, with the caveat that "care must be taken that the lectures are accommodated to the capacity of the students" (*Letter to Father John Pelletier*, 1551, in Young, p. 246). Understanding Latin, however, was not the only condition for language acquisition. In a letter in which Ignatius explains the foundation of colleges and the benefits to be derived from them, he also describes how students are to be instructed in Latin:

> The names of all these pupils are taken in writing, and care is taken not only that they attend the diverse lectures, but also that they be made to exercise themselves in disputations, compositions, and in speaking Latin constantly, in such a way that they make much progress in letters and virtues alike (*Letter to Father Antonio Araoz*, 1551, in Ganss 1954, p. 26).

Interpretive skills can be acquired by comprehending the lectures, but expressive skills must be cultivated by using the language to exchange ideas. Ignatius recommends that students meet in small groups after the lecture to discuss its content "with one [student] repeating [the content of the lecture] and the others listening, and with mutual proposing of difficult points; and that they go to their teachers if there is something that they cannot settle among themselves" (*Constitutions*; Part IV, in Fitzpatrick 1933, pp. 74-75). Language ability would develop as the message of the day's lesson was negotiated by the learners in a small group setting. They were encouraged to solve problems together as best as they could, using the teacher as a resource.

Active engagement in communicative language use was to be the preferred method of instruction, "al modo de París, con mucho exercitio" [in the way of Paris, with great activity] (Ganss 1954, p. 324). Because of his belief that second language development proceeds through meaningful interaction, Ignatius repeatedly recommends students' participation in discussion and composition. Both daily and weekly debates were to be held within each class, as well as in front of the entire school (Fitzpatrick 1933, pp. 74-75; *Constitutions*, Part IV, Chapters 6, 13, 16; in Ganss 1954, pp. 303, 323-324, 330).

Use of the second language, however, was not limited to the classroom setting. Like Guarino and other early Italian humanists, Ignatius advocates total immersion in the second language. He insists that "all, but especially the students of humane letters, should ordinarily speak Latin" (Fitzpatrick 1933, p. 76; *Constitutions*, Part IV, Chapters 6; in Ganss 1954, p. 304). The teacher's role was to encourage learners' active use of Latin, in and out of class. The teacher should make sure "that the students of the classical language cultivate their ordinary conversation by speaking Latin commonly; and their style, by writing" (*Constitutions*, Part IV, Chapter 13, in Fitzpatrick 1933, p. 103).

It was the teacher's job to provide content that students would find interesting and motivating in the second language. They were also to encourage students to interact with that content. In turn, it was the student's responsibility to "be faithful in attendance at the lectures, diligent in preparing for them beforehand, and afterwards in reviewing them. They must ask about points they do not understand, and note down what may be useful later on to assist the memory" (*Constitutions*, Part IV, Chapter 6, in Ganss 1954, p. 302). Students must take an active role in the language learning process.

In addition to the interactive use of Latin in daily tasks and encounters, Ignatius acknowledges that different contexts of language use call for different kinds of skills. He observes that:

> After dinner on Sunday or some other designated day, they [the students of humanities] should defend theses or exercise themselves in writing compositions in prose or in verse. They may compose these extemporaneously as a test of facility, or they may bring something already written and read it publicly there (*Constitutions*, Part IV, Chapter 6, in Ganss, pp. 303-304).

The development of oral and written fluency was prized, but not above the ideas expressed. In addition to the daily discussion and weekly debates required of all students, Ignatius also recommends that:

> After dinner on some day of each week, one of the more advanced students should deliver a Latin or Greek oration, about some subject likely to edify the members of the community and the externs, and to animate them to greater perfection in our Lord (*Constitutions*, Part IV, Chapter 6, in Ganss, p. 304).

In a curriculum that combined subject-matter competence and language, highly-developed expressive skills are desirable, but the content of the message must necessarily take precedence over its style. Displays of erudition should not exceed the limits of propriety. Ignatius does not subscribe to the belief that fluency and ostentation are compatible. He reacts to the style of a letter written by Father Robert Clayssone in the following way:

> While your letter is in some respects ornate and learned, we miss a becoming modesty in the ornament used and in the show of learning. It is one thing to be eloquent and charming in profane speech, and another when the one who is speaking is a religious. Just as in a matron that ornament which is modest and chaste is to be commended, so in the style which Ours should use when speaking or writing we do not look for what is wanton or adolescent, but for a style that is dignified and mature. This is especially so in letters, where the writing by its very nature must be more compact and polished and manifest at the same time an abundance of ideas rather than of words. (*Letter to Father Robert Clayssone*, 1555, in Young, p. 376)

Written communication should be "compact and polished," but attention to form must never override the significance of the message. Ideas are more important than words.

Because the plan was to train students "both in letters and good morals" (*Constitutions*, Part IV, Chapter 7, in Ganss 1954, p. 308), Ignatius advises that "it will be good to have some of the more advanced among the students carefully compose some Latin discourses on the Christian virtues" in order to "have them declaim them publicly in the presence of all, on Sundays and feast days" (*Letter to Father John Pelletier*, 1551, in Young, p. 247). In this way, all students, future Jesuits or not, would "absorb along with their letters the morals worthy of a Christian" (*Constitutions*, Part IV, Chapter 7, in Ganss 1954, p. 308). Because language and content are acquired simultaneously, careful attention is paid to the selection of the texts. The content of texts was scrutinized, and objectionable texts were omitted.

Within Ignatius's pedagogy, Latin is a fully functional language in both oral and written forms. It primarily conveys meaning: It transmits moral messages as well as historical facts and rhetorical figures. The second language is the medium of communication across all contexts of use: from the most casual and private interactions among peers to formal public performances. Neither is it purely an artifact to be studied, nor is its use relegated to only one, academic, context.

Language and letters (including rhetoric, poetry, and history) formed the core content of the college curriculum. Ignatius intended that all students in the Jesuit college be taught using the humanist method. How long would it take a student to complete such a course of study? It took from four "in the case of beginners of good ability" to six years (*Constitutions*, Part IV, Chapter 15, in Ganss, p. 327). Ignatius is well aware that the rate of language development varies widely among learners. He states that "in the study of humane letters and the languages there cannot be a set period of time for their completion, because of the difference in abilities and learning of those who hear the lectures, and because of other reasons too" (*Constitutions*, Part IV, Chapter 15, in Ganss, p. 327). Therefore, how will the terms of the Jesuit college be calculated? It is done only on a case-by-case basis because "these [reasons] permit no other prescription of time save that which the prudent consideration of the rector or chancellor will arrange for each student [as] no definite rule can be given" (*Constitutions*, Part IV, Chapter 15, in Ganss, p. 327).

Upon completion of the *studia humanitatis* students possessed a solid preparation for study in the "arts:" logic, philosophy, and metaphysics; and then theology and Scripture. The curriculum also constituted the best kind of education for young people who would not go on to advanced study. It was a pedagogy based on the use of rich and interesting second language texts: oral texts, in the form of lectures, discussions, and debates; written texts, in the form of original compositions and summaries, in addition to the classical authors.

---

*P*ause to consider . . .

that Ignatius emphasizes that students progress at their own rates; therefore, no precise timetable for language acquisition can be prescribed. How is the rate of language development still an issue in the contemporary debate regarding "seat time" and proficiency requirements?

The Role of the Vernacular According to Ignatius

No doubt Ignatius's own intensely practical nature, in combination with his years of real-world experience in the military and at court, contributed to the keen sense of pragmatism that pervades his writing. As convinced as he was of the benefits of the humanist curriculum for learning Latin, he could not ignore the role of the vernacular in the students' lives. Because of it, Ignatius recommends that students, especially those who intend to become priests, perfect their expressive skills in the vernacular. Because students were already fluent in their mother tongue, not more than an hour a week was deemed sufficient exercise. Such practice was limited to oral skills, for the purpose of addressing the uneducated general populace in sermons.

Situations in which the language of the wider community was a foreign language posed a special problem. In a letter to Father Manual Lopez in regard to a member's work in Germany, Ignatius writes: "It is difficult to help them otherwise than by training laborers who speak their own language

[German]" (*Letter to Father Manuel Lopez*, 1555, in Young, p. 394). In a letter to the rectors of the Society, Polanco writes, in Ignatius's name:

> It seems to be required for the benefit and edification of the peoples among whom our Society is living and for the increase of union and charity and kindliness among Ours, that in places where we have a college or a house *all who do not know the language which is in common use should learn it and as a rule speak it.* If each spoke his mother tongue, there would be much confusion and lack of union, seeing that we are of different nations. For this reason our father [Ignatius] has given orders that in all places where the Society exists, all of Ours should speak the language of that country. In Spain, Spanish; in France, French; in Germany, German; in Italy, Italian; and so on (*Letter to the Rectors of the Society*, 1556, in Young, pp. 412-413; emphasis mine).

The regulation to learn and speak the vernacular of the community in which the Jesuits worked is noteworthy because it is unequivocal. The occasions in which Ignatius gives orders are rare. Typically, he is careful to allow the possibility of adapting his recommendations according to particular circumstances of persons and places. In this instance he is not. Latin was no longer the language of wider communication in sixteenth-century Europe.

Strategies for Success from an Administrator par excellence

Ignatius was a savvy administrator. He knew when to hold the line and when to allow for slack. He also gave astute advice for how the colleges would be funded. First, not surprisingly, he recommends sacrifice and prayer. He also seems to suggest that former students, grateful for the education they have received, might be a source of support. He then outlines the following five strategies for financial success:

(1) "Try to preserve and increase the good will of the prince;"
(2) "Make an effort to win over individuals and benefactors, talk with them on spiritual things;"
(3) "You should try if possible to have our friends rather than ourselves ask for us and manage our temporal affairs, or let it be done in such a way that there is not even the appearance of greed;"
(4) "Acquire real estate near the center of the city;" and,
(5) "Write us every week for help and guidance" (*Letter to Father John Pelletier*, 1551, in Young, 248-249).

In other words, a strong alumni association, friends in high places, professional management, a choice location, and good communication would ensure the future of the colleges—along with God's help, of course.

Fundraising and public relations aside, the adept administrator explains the importance of delegation of work within the Society, citing himself as an example:

> It is not the duty of the provincial, nor of the general, to take into account the minute details of affairs. Even if he had the greatest possible ability to do so, it would be better to entrust such details to others, who can later report to the provincial on what they have done, and he will determine, after hearing what they have to say, whatever it is his business to determine. If it is something the handling and decision of which he can leave to others, it would be better for him to do so, especially in temporal matters, and even in many that are spiritual. This is my own practice (*Letter to Father James Miron*, 1552, in Young, p. 279).

Not one to ignore his own advice, Ignatius acknowledges that the system of education that he has laid out in the *Constitutions* still lacks detail. He delegates the responsibility of working out the particulars to others:

> Concerning the hours of the lectures, their order, and their method, and concerning the exercises both in compositions (which ought to be corrected by the teachers) and in disputations within all the faculties, and those of delivering orations and reading verses in public—all this will be treated in detail in a separate treatise. This present *Constitution* refers its readers to it, with the remark that it ought to be adapted to places, times, and persons (*Constitutions*, Part IV, Chapter 13, in Ganss 1954, p. 323).

Coupled with a frank understanding of human nature, Ignatius's practicality is apparent throughout his writing, in his recommendations for language teaching and for school administration. He realizes the importance of tailoring his plan to individual colleges. He advocates the institution of rules for each college, according to circumstances of place and persons. However, he does not leave the interpretation of what is essential in his teaching plan to chance. As if to underline what constitutes the core of that vision, Ignatius sums up the overriding characteristics of the method to be followed:

> There should be not only lectures which are delivered in public, but also different masters, according to the capacity and number of the students. These masters should take an interest in the progress of each one of their students. They should require them to give an account of their lessons and to repeat them. They should make those who are studying the humanities get practice of ordinarily speaking Latin, by composing, and by delivering well what they have composed. They should make them—and much more those studying the

higher branches—engage frequently in disputations. Days and times should be designated for this. At these times, their disputations should not be only with their fellow classmen, but those who are somewhat lower down should dispute about matters they understand with students who are more advanced, and those who are more advanced should debate with those lower down by taking subjects which these latter are studying. The professors, too, ought to dispute with one another, but care should always be taken to preserve the proper modesty. Someone should preside who is to close the debate and sum up the doctrine (*Constitutions*, Part IV, Chapter 13, in Ganss, pp. 323-324).

Ignatius envisioned a network of colleges in which the *studia humanitatis* formed the whole curriculum. What did the bare bones of the approach entail? First, all communication should take place in the second language, Latin. Second, instruction should consist of interaction with second language texts, oral and written. In this way, language and content would be learned simultaneously. Interpretive and expressive skills would develop as a natural consequence of using Latin to convey meaning. At all levels, everyone, from the youngest pupil to the most experienced professor, would engage in the discussion of interesting subject matter in Latin. The instructional goal of attaining functional second language competence then would be met.

The theory of second language learning and teaching that underlies Ignatius's plan for the Jesuit college parallels that of Guarino. If this then served as the model for the large-scale implementation of the humanist curriculum in the Jesuit colleges, colleges that spread and educated generations of intellectuals, then why isn't it the model to which one normally refers when speaking of "traditional" language teaching? Why does "traditional" language teaching recall Battista's treatise instead? Actually, Ignatius's plan is not the one that formed the basis of the Jesuit curriculum. A different plan was followed, one which attempted to convert Ignatius's beliefs into a method. On the way towards institutionalization, Ignatius's theory too, like Guarino's, was altered, and in that process something of his vision was lost.

---

*P*ause to consider . . .

the model for second language acquisition proposed by Guarino and Ignatius and that which is contemporarily known as "content-based instruction," in which students learn subject-area knowledge through the medium of second language. How are they similar?

IN OTHERS' WORDS: IGNATIUS'S VISION REVISITED IN THE RATIO STUDIORUM

The *Ratio Studiorum* [Plan of Study] is the characteristic document of the Jesuit system of education. The formulation of the *Ratio* began in 1584, 32 years after the publication of Ignatius's *Constitutions*, and it was formally issued in 1599, 43 years after Ignatius's death. It contains the details that Ignatius admittedly did not include in his own plan. It also is a document distinguished for its pedantry. How and by whom was the document prepared? And why did it take so long?

The relationship between the *Constitutions* and the *Ratio* shed some light on the matter. The *Ratio* was not the product of a single author, or even a fixed group of authors. Rather, it represents a consensus of the experience and judgment of various rectors, teachers, and members of the Society. In 1581, twelve Jesuits were named to form a commission dedicated to the preparation of the details that Ignatius had recommended in the Fourth Part of the *Constitutions*. Nothing developed. In 1584, Father Aquaviva, the fifth general of the Society, called six experienced Jesuit educators to Rome to complete the same charge. The group met, studied, and discussed the matter for nine months. A draft of their report went out to all the professors in the Jesuit college in Rome. Aquaviva and his assistants also read, discussed, and commented on the draft. Changes were made based on the feedback, and a revised version went out to the provinces for further comments. In each province, a committee of five was formed to study the draft and report their reactions.

The preliminary version of the *Ratio* of 1586 contained lengthy discussions of pedagogical questions. According to Fitzpatrick (1933), it included "the statement not only of the methods or directions to be included in the final plan, but also the reasoning and principles upon which they were based" (p. 31). At this point, General Aquaviva made an administrative decision: Notification was sent along with the 1586 draft that only the directions for method and the rules to be followed would be included in the final plan. Again, the professors of the Roman college, members of the 1585-86 committee, Aquaviva, and his assistants reviewed the document. Another version of the plan, the *Ratio atque Institutio Studiorum* of 1591 containing only the rules —for everyone from teachers in the lowest grades to the rector, prefect, and provincial—was sent to the provinces. The preface called for a three-year study of the draft.

After two years, a report on the plan was presented at the fifth general congregation of the Society. The assembly lobbied for a shorter version. The matter was again studied by Aquaviva and the Roman college. The final version containing half the number of pages of the 1591 version became definitive in 1599. It would not be revised again until 1832.

The amount of feedback and revision that apparently accompanied the preparation of the *Ratio* has convinced some scholars that it represents "a consensus of judgment" in which "unity was secured in the mutual rein-forcement of curriculum, method, and school administration" (Fitzpatrick 1933, p. 27). Whereas the *Constitutions* reflect Ignatius's theory of education, the *Ratio* is considered "a practical handbook in educational method and school and class management" (Fitzpatrick, p. 31). Despite the late date of its completion, it was asserted that the *Ratio* reflects the spirit and genius of Ignatius of Loyola's beliefs regarding education, especially as evidenced in the Fourth Part of his *Constitutions of the Society of Jesus* (Ganss 1954). How-ever, a comparison of the *Ratio Studiorum of 1599* with the ideas expressed by Ignatius in his letters and *Constitutions* casts doubt upon the accuracy of that claim, especially with regard to second language instruction.

Lest anyone believe that the *Ratio* was composed hastily or without due consideration of its import, the "Letter of Transmission," which serves as a preamble to the *Ratio*, explains the reason for the delay in its publication:

> For it was proper, in a matter so important and involved in so many difficulties, not to determine anything before the objections and the demands of the provinces should be carefully examined, so that as far as possible all might be satisfied and so that the work which here-after ought to be put into practice by all should be more favorably received ("Letter of Transmission" in the *Ratio Studiorum of 1599*, in Fitzpatrick 1933, p. 119).

What was done to satisfy everyone and ensure their cooperation in the implementation of the plan? The *Ratio* was reduced to a set of straightfor-ward rules: Because "the majority preferred above all else greater brevity in this plan [...], it was decided what should be firmly established and all things as far as possible were reduced to a shorter and more convenient method" ("Letter of Transmission," in Fitzpatrick, p. 120). All justifications and expla-nations were omitted. The final version of the *Ratio* contained the "how" but not the "why." Could it be that teachers had begged, "Just tell us what to do on Monday morning"? Or did Aquaviva and his assistants decide that this was all teachers and administrators needed to know? The historical records cannot answer that question; however, given Ignatius's propensity for expla-nation and justification, it is clear that it was a decision he would not have made.

To reiterate the definitive nature of the plan, the readers of the Ratio are reminded that all previous versions are null and void:

> Wherefore, this plan of studies which is now sent ought to be observed in the future by all of ours, setting aside all other plans which heretofore had been sent for the sake of experiment, and the careful effort of our doctors should be fixed on this that what is pre-scribed in this final *Ratio* should be put into execution readily and cheerfully ("Letter of Transmission," in Fitzpatrick, p. 120).

Just in case the implementation is less than "cheerful," the preamble makes clear that this document should not be perceived as a mere set of suggestions. Everyone's strict adherence to it is demanded:

> Very Reverend Father General [Aquaviva] seriously and earnestly commands that they [the superiors] strive with as great zeal as possible that this matter which is so much commended in our *Constitutions*, and which it is believed will bring such rich advantages to all our students, be carried out readily and exactly ("Letter of Transmission," in Fitzpatrick, pp. 120-121).

From the outset, Ignatius's concern that time, place, circumstances, and individuals always be taken into account has fallen by the wayside. *This* plan must "be carried out readily and exactly" by everyone, without deviation or exception. It is a command that is repeated throughout the document.

Ignatius himself had recommended that someone else work out all the particulars of his plan. That is precisely what the *Ratio* purports to do. The following directions for determining vacation periods give the reader an idea of the level of precision found in the *Ratio*. The passage is prefaced once again by the admonition that the rules be strictly followed:

> Just as earnestness is necessary in literary exercises, so is some vacation important; still, care must be taken that no new vacations be introduced, and that those which are prescribed be carefully observed. On this point, the following directions must be given ("Rules for the Provincial," *Ratio*, in Fitzpatrick, p. 135).

Specific days and times for vacations take up the next two pages of text. Interestingly, lower classes (younger pupils) receive less vacation than higher classes. However, the amount of detail provided is excruciating. For example, weekly vacation is determined according to the following rules:

> At least one day each week shall be allowed for rest. But if two feast days fall during the same week, there shall be no other day of vacation; unless perchance, as often happens, one of them falls on Saturday, the other on Monday; then another day may be granted. But if there is one feast day during the week, and it falls on Wednesday or Thursday, there shall be vacation on that day and no other; but if it falls on Saturday or Monday, there shall also be vacation on Wednesday or Thursday; if it falls on Tuesday or Friday, then if there is no sermon and the time may be given for recreation, then there shall be another day of vacation on Wednesday or Thursday (*Ratio*, in Fitzpatrick, p. 136).

Further qualifications apply, specifying whether the vacation day would consist of an entire day, the afternoon only, or part of the morning as well, according to the level of the class and whether it is summer. The fastidiousness of the text, punctuated by a litany of self-correcting "buts" is overwhelming.

The level of specification found in the previous passage is not anomalous. Equally precise rules are given for how to conduct examinations, award prizes, practice disputations, correct papers, and lecture. Moreover, they are presented in separate sections for each level of administration. There are chapters of rules for the provincial and the rector, one for the prefect of studies (assistant to the rector), and another for the professor of theology. The rules continue, all the way down the hierarchy to the teacher of the highest course of grammar, the middle course, the lowest course, and, finally, the janitor. Rules are given even for how often the teachers should meet to review the rules! This consists of at least once a month for the teachers of grammar. Each chapter addressed to a teacher begins in the same way: with a warning to stick only to one's own subject matter, and to do everything "for the greater glory of God."

Perhaps it is unfair to criticize the *Ratio*'s authoritative stance without first looking at the details that pertain to language teaching.

Latin and the Vernacular, Again: Using the First Language to Mediate the Second

As for the practice of using Latin as the ordinary means of communication among students and teachers alike, the *Ratio* describes, in detail, who is to use Latin and when. Primarily, it is the duty of the rector—

> —to see to it that the use of Latin is diligently preserved among the Scholastics [future Jesuits]; there shall be no exception from this rule of speaking Latin except on days of vacation and in hours of recreation [...] that when those of the Order who have not yet finished their studies write to other members of the Order, they shall write in Latin. Moreover, two or three times a year, when some celebration is held, such as at the recommencement of studies or the renewal of vows, both the philosophy and theology students shall prepare and post verses" (*Ratio*, in Fitzpatrick, p. 139).

In sharp contrast to Ignatius's view that everyone be constantly immersed in Latin, the *Ratio* drastically curtails its use. Latin was no longer required "ordinarily" and of "all." Students only used it while they were in class. Latin is used for written communication, but only between advanced students and fellow Jesuits, and what Ignatius had recommended as a weekly opportunity to practice formal oral skills had become a twice yearly exercise in the use of written verse. Elsewhere in the document similar caveats on the use of the second language are found. Latin is often recommended, but it is not required. For example, among the beginning students, the professors of the lower classes are reminded to "let the practice of speaking Latin be especially strictly guarded *excepting in those classes in which the pupils do not know*

Latin; so that it never is allowed to use the vernacular *in any matter which pertains to class*" (*Ratio, Rules Common to the Professors of the Lower Classes*, in Fitzpatrick, pp. 198-199, emphasis mine). Students in the lower classes then were allowed to use the vernacular because they didn't "know" Latin. The idea that they might acquire Latin by using it is nonexistent. In any case, even if they were to possess enough of the second language to communicate, these students were required to use Latin only in their academic work.

Further proof that Latin was no longer a fully functional language in the college can be found in the directive that immediately succeeds the rule on speaking Latin: "Black marks even being given in class if any neglect this; and for this reason let the master always use the Latin language" (*Ratio, Rules Common to the Professors of the Lower Classes*, in Fitzpatrick, p. 199). The "black marks" were given by the decurians, slightly more advanced students who acted as teacher aides and snitches, continuing the practice of the "lupi" [wolves] common in the medieval university system who reported those who spoke in the vernacular instead of in Latin. Why were "black marks" and spies necessary? How did Latin become a forced and artificial language in the classroom, instead of the normal means of communication? A closer look at the curriculum provides the answer.

*P*ause to consider . . .

the possible effects of using the students' first languages for everyday social interaction and "important" messages (e.g., instructions and announcements of exam dates) and reserving the second language for "practice" speaking, drill, and study. What impression would students have of the function of the second language?

The Three Rs: Rules, Review, and (No) Respect

In his plan, Ignatius had advocated three instructional practices: All communication would take place in Latin; the curriculum would be based on interesting oral and written second language texts; and students would interact with each other and their teachers about the content of the texts. Grammar—that is, how language works—would be acquired in this manner. In other words, using the language to learn results in language learning. This was the humanists' method. The *Ratio*, conversely, delineates the curriculum as follows: "There should not be more than five grades of lower studies (leaving out the ABC classes, for reasons stated in the Fourth Part of the *Constitutions*), one of rhetoric, a second of humanities, and three of grammar" (*Ratio, Rules for the Provincial*, in Fitzpatrick, p. 130). In the system described by the *Ratio*, humanities and grammar are no longer co-extensive. If Latin were not to be acquired through the study of the classical authors, then how would it be taught? Thanks to the specificity of the *Ratio* what the three years of grammar instruction looked like is not left to the imagination.

Rather than relying on the classical authors to provide models of language use, the *Ratio* emphasizes the explicit teaching and learning of rules. The grammar of Emmanuel or the "Roman" one (perhaps Donatus, the most popular grammar text of the medieval period) functioned as the core text for the "grammar" classes. What is important about the choice of a grammar book is that it preserve "the force and the propriety of all the precepts of Emmanuel" (*Ratio*, in Fitzpatrick, p. 132). From the start, Latin was viewed as a system of precepts, not as a system of communication. The rules contained in the grammar are divided into three books, one to be covered in each year of grammar:

> That this distinction [between grades] may be better and more easily preserved, all rules of Emmanuel must be divided into three books, of which each is appropriate to a single class.
>
> The first book for the lowest class will contain the first book of Emmanuel, and a brief introduction to syntax taken from the second book.
>
> The second book for the middle class will contain the second book of Emmanuel on the construction of the eight parts of speech up to figured speech taking in addition the more easy appendices.
>
> The third book for the highest class will contain from the second book the appendices of the second class and from figured construction to the end, and the third book which treats about the measuring of syllables. (*Ratio, Rules for the Prefect of Lower Studies*, in Fitzpatrick, pp. 177-178).

The attempt to teach language through the explicit teaching of rules created more than a little difficulty. Because students did not learn the rules on the first pass through, they needed to continually revisit them. Thus, recapitulation of the previous grade's material was built into the curriculum. In fact, review began within the same academic year: "The master practically completes the book of each class during the first semester, and begins from the beginning in the second" (Ratio, in Fitzpatrick, p. 178). The practice of repeating the grammar in the same year served two purposes: remediation and acceleration. The students who did not understand the material the first time around got a second chance at it—an implicit admission of the ineffectiveness of instruction. They got a third chance when it was reviewed again at the beginning of the following year. Conversely, any student who succeeded in memorizing the rules on the initial try could jump to the next class, completing the grammar curriculum in half the time, and so progress rapidly to higher studies.

However, in addition to the inability of most students to master the rules, the *Ratio* acknowledges that there were simply too many rules to be learned! The problem begins in the first class:

Since, however, the book of the lowest class is larger than can be completed and reviewed entirely in one year, it is accordingly divided into two parts. And indeed it would be better not to admit boys unless they be well trained in the first part, so that the second part may be completed and reviewed in the one year, as is the case in other classes (*Ratio, Rules for the Prefect of Lower Studies*, in Fitzpatrick, p. 178).

---

*P**ause to consider . . .*

the similarities and differences between first- and second-year language textbooks. Compare the table of contents of a first-year language textbook with that of a second-year book. To what extent do they share the same grammatical syllabus? What purpose is served by the overlap?

The *Ratio* reinstated the medieval focus on language learning as the memorization of rules. This orientation was advantageous to a system that sought to group students according to clearly delineated grades. The textbook could be divided among the three grammar classes, with review built in to bridge the transition from one level to the next. The division of instructional content was based on administrative concerns: how much teachers could teach, the structure of the school year (semesters), and the problem of articulation between classes. However, the neat structure that resulted from the change in focus contradicted at least two of Ignatius's beliefs: (1), that a timetable for language learning cannot be set due to idiosyncratic rates of acquisition among learners; and, (2), that the only prerequisites for admission to college be knowledge of the ABC's and the parents' permission.

Because it raised the entrance requirement from a familiarity with the alphabet to some degree of grammatical competence in Latin, the *Ratio* pushed the responsibility for teaching language to a lower level of instruction. In doing so, certain kinds of studies were perceived as more important or more scholarly, than were language classes. This might seem to be a subtle, almost imperceptible shift; instead, it reflects a pervasive lack of esteem for language teaching that Ignatius had vainly attempted to dispel. In fact, language teaching was held in such low regard that when Father Lainez proposed a punishment for himself, he suggested possible penances, the following being the most severe:

Relieve me of the care of others, take away my preaching and my study, leaving me only my breviary, and bid me come to Rome, begging my way, and there put me to work in the kitchen, or serving table, or in the garden, or at anything else. *And when I am no longer good for any of this, put me in the lowest class of grammar and that until death, without any more care for me [...] than you have for an old broom* (*Letter to Ignatius from Lainez*, 1552, in Young, p. 273, emphasis mine).

In a religious order that valued intellectual ability above all others, disdain for language teaching was rampant. The *Ratio* repeatedly states the difficulty in finding and retaining grammar teachers. Advanced students who intended to become Jesuits were required to spend a couple of years teaching in the lower divisions. In fact, the constant flux of grammar teachers is used as justification for the rigid methodology found in the *Ratio*. In a rare instance of explanation, the *Ratio* states that strict adherence to one plan "gives outsiders less justification for condemning our frequent change of teachers" (*Ratio, Rules for the Prefect of Lower Studies*, in Fitzpatrick 1933, p. 176). In fact, Ignatius's concern for beginning students is not conveyed anywhere in the *Ratio*.

The norm in the Jesuit college was five grades: three of grammar, one of humanities, and one of rhetoric. However, in case resources are lacking, the *Ratio* recommends that either rhetoric be omitted, or better yet, that rhetoric become the highest class after grammar, and that humanities move up to the next level of instruction. If only three grades were to be offered, then two would be of grammar and the third would be "pure humanities" or a combination of humanities and rhetoric (*Ratio, Rules for the Prefect of Lower Studies*, in Fitzpatrick, p. 179). If only two grades were possible, then one would suffice for beginning and intermediate grammar and the second would consist of advanced grammar and humanities (*Ratio*; in Fitzpatrick, pp. 179-80). Paradoxically, the grammar rules, which were considered too abundant for a three-year course of study, could be condensed to fit into half the amount of time, when needed. The directions to the superiors are blunt: "Care must be taken, whenever there are fewer classes, that the higher ones be retained as far as possible and the lower ones dropped" (*Ratio, Rules for the Provincial*, in Fitzpatrick, p. 130). As language instruction centered ever more tightly on the study of rules, content moved out of the reach of the beginning and intermediate students. Humanities, once the mainstay, were reserved for the advanced students.

---

*P*ause to consider . . .

to what extent an institutional bias against beginning-level language courses still exists in the university. Who teaches beginning language courses? How much recognition, value, and prestige are conferred on such teachers and courses?

Telling Teachers What to Do on Monday Morning, Tuesday Morning, Wednesday . . .

Although Ignatius makes almost no mention of the study of language structure, *per se*, it is a point that is raised repeatedly throughout the *Ratio*, especially in the chapters of rules for the teachers of grammar. Everything is specified, from the grammar texts that are to be used to the division of grammatical topics throughout the curriculum. For the lowest grammar class, the instructional objective is "the perfect knowledge of the rudiments and a beginning knowledge of syntax, if it begins with the declensions up to the [fourteen rules of] construction of the common verbs" (*Ratio, Rules for the Professor of Lower Grammar Classes*, in Fitzpatrick, p. 230). The goal of the middle class is "the knowledge, indeed, of the whole of grammar, but less exhaustively [than the higher class]" (*Ratio, Rules for the Professor of Middle Grammar Classes*, in Fitzpatrick, p. 226). Finally, in the highest class, the student shall have "a complete knowledge of grammar; for he shall so repeat syntax from the beginning as to add all the appendices, and then explain figured construction and the art of versification" (*Ratio, Rules for the Professor of Higher Grammar Classes*, in Fitzpatrick, p. 222). Just as in Battista's treatise, the language surrounding a focus on rules is rich with absolutes: from the very beginning, students' knowledge of rules must be "perfect."

The pedagogy for the treatment of grammar is described in detail. The lesson plans are similar for each class. In the morning during the first hour, students recite from memory passages from Cicero and the grammar book to the decurians—those slightly more advanced students who served as teachers' aides for groups of ten students—while the teacher corrects the written work and assigns exercises. The exercises involve translating sentences from Latin to the vernacular (in the lower classes) or from the vernacular to Latin (in the higher). During the second hour, the last lecture is reviewed and the new one presented. A dictation may follow. Finally, a new grammar point is presented. The afternoon lesson is spent on Greek in the higher grammar class. In the lower and middle classes, students recite from memory rules of Latin grammar, further explanations of grammar are given, and "a little more than a quarter of an hour" is spent on Greek grammar (*Ratio*, in Fitzpatrick, p. 232).

Clearly, most of the students' time was spent memorizing sentences, reciting grammar rules, and translating to and from the vernacular. The vernacular appears to have crept into the curriculum, even though Ignatius had advocated the sole use of the second language for all communication. To what extent was Latin the medium of instruction as well as the object? Were the students at least listening to "lectures in Latin, with care taken that they be adjusted to the ability of the learners" as Ignatius had proposed?

In fact, the vernacular began to displace Latin throughout the lessons. The directions for the lectures reveal that students hear as much in the vernacular as in Latin. The *Ratio* provides the following procedure for how teachers in the first grammar classes were to present the lecture:

> The prelection [lecture] in Cicero which shall not exceed four lines will be in this form: First, let him [the teacher] read the entire passage continuously, and state its topic very briefly in the vernacular. Second, let him express the sentence in words of the vernacular. Third, starting from the beginning, let him indicate the structure and explain the sentence, telling which words govern which cases; let him go over many things pertaining to the laws of the grammar already explained; let him offer some observations or other of the Latin language, but as simple as possible; let him explain the metaphors by well-known examples, but let him not dictate anything, except perhaps the topic. Fourth, let him again go through the words of the author in the vernacular (*Ratio, Rules to the Professor of Lower Grammar Classes*, in Fitzpatrick, p. 233).

The lectures, like the written exercises, consisted of line-by-line translation. The content of the text was transmitted through the vernacular, not Latin. The use of translation to transmit meaning stands in sharp contrast to Ignatius's and Guarino's belief that content can be successfully conveyed in the second language to even complete novices, when teachers adjust their speech to the level of the learners. Instead, the prescription found in the *Ratio* is consistent with the belief that beginning learners, because they do not know the rules of the language, are not able to use the language for any purpose.

The directions for the lectures in the second-year class reveal little change in procedure. The only difference is in the number of lines to be read—seven instead of four—and the use of dictation:

> The prelections [lectures] in Cicero which generally will not exceed seven lines each time, will be in this form: First let him [the teacher] read the entire passage continuously, and state its topic very briefly in the vernacular. Second, let him express the sentence in words of the vernacular. Third, starting from the beginning, let him indicate the structure and explain the sentence, telling which words govern which cases; let him go over many things pertaining to the laws of grammar already explained; let him offer some observation or other in Latin, but as simply as possible; let him explain the metaphors by well-known examples; let him select some phrase or other, which he shall dictate along with the topic. Fourth, let him again go through the words of the author in the vernacular (*Ratio, Rules to the Professor of Middle Grammar Classes*, in Fitzpatrick, p. 229).

Even in the second year, students did not access meaning directly from the Latin; they relied on the vernacular. What of the final third year of grammar, during which students purportedly acquired a "complete knowledge of the grammar"? The directions remain remarkably unchanged:

> First he [the teacher] will go through the subject both in Latin and in the vernacular; secondly he will so interpret each sentence that the vernacular explanation will be given immediately after the Latin; in the third place going through it again from the beginning (unless he wishes to insert this in the explanation), he will select words by twos and threes of which he will explain the force and the derivation (*Ratio, Rules to the Professor of Higher Grammar Classes*, in Fitzpatrick, p. 224).

Again, the only difference between the lecture in the higher class and the middle and lower classes was the length of the passage and the grammar focus. It may seem obvious that students who receive a translation of every message in their mother tongue would have no incentive to listen to it in the second language. The practice of translation, while certainly conveying the content of the lecture, produces no interpretative competence in a second language. Because the *Ratio* was based on the consensus of experienced language teachers, what is clear from these directions is that even after three years of intensive daily exposure to grammar rules, students still could not use those rules to interpret oral text. Therefore, the lectures that Ignatius had intended to use to provide exposure to oral discourse in the second language had become reading followed by word-for-word translation. The performance of the classical authors' texts with animation, intonation, breath marks, gesture, and other cues to meaning had been reduced to grammar explanations, and an insistence on rules.

If Latin were not the medium of communication for even the lectures and if thoughts were not conveyed to the students through Latin, what chance would exist that they would use Latin to convey their ideas to others? That Latin was not used for communication had a devastating effect on Ignatius's recommendation that interaction would improve students' expressive skills.

It isn't that the authors of the *Ratio* ignored completely Ignatius's charge that activity accompany language learning. The *Ratio* prescribes a particular type of interaction among students: the concertatio. This activity consists of students ferreting out errors in each other's written work, pointing them out, and demanding a repetition of the rule that was broken. For example, in the case of an incorrect word ending, a recitation of "the whole declension or conjugation in order or in broken order, alone or with an adjective or noun or pronoun" may be asked of a beginning student (*Ratio, Rules to the Professor of Lower Grammar Classes*; in Fitzpatrick, p. 234). The concertatio is recommended for all students of grammar, again only the focus of the grammar correction changes according to the level of the students. Because it deals with written work and grammar rules that appeared in their texts, the concertatio is a rare exercise that the *Ratio* advises to be conducted in Latin: "Seeing that one who is asked a question replies at once in the same words and, with a little mediation, answers in Latin, not verbatim, but at least in entirety" (*Ratio, Rules to the Professor of Higher Grammar Classes*, in Fitzpatrick, p. 226).

Psittacism, the repetition of memorized phrases, in classroom activities, compositions, and literary imitation is a practice scorned by the humanists. Instead, Ignatius had proposed small group discussions of the day's lecture among students "with mutual proposing of difficult points"(*Constitutions*, Part IV, in Fitzpatrick pp. 20-21). This activity is recorded in the *Ratio* as follows:

> After the lecture, let him [the teacher] remain in the classroom or near the classroom for at least a quarter of an hour so that the students may approach him to ask questions, so that he may sometimes ask an account of the lectures, and so that the lectures may be repeated (*Ratio, Common Rules for All Professors of Higher Faculties*, in Fitzpatrick, p. 152).

Missing is any reference to students' interactions with each other and their negotiation of the subject matter. The spontaneous, free discussion suggested by Ignatius is transformed by the *Ratio* into a quiz session. The role of the teacher has shifted from that of a resource to be contacted as a last resort to the dominant character. Not only are the small group sessions unrecognizable, the discussions and more formal disputations have also mutated.

Rather than a lively exchange of ideas and arguments at the conclusion of which the teacher sums up the essential doctrine, the disputations, too, become advanced exercises in form: "From the very beginning of logic let the young men be so trained that nothing would make them more ashamed than to fail in the form of disputation. And let the instructor demand nothing more severely from them than the laws and the method of disputing" (*Ratio, Rules for the Professor of Philosophy*, in Fitzpatrick, p. 174). Furthermore, active participation is limited to the best of the advanced students: "for the general disputations only those of exceptional talent and ability should be selected" (*Ratio, Rules for the Prefect of Studies*, in Fitzpatrick, p. 145). Teachers are instructed to be concerned with the form of the disputation, the "laws and the method," but no mention is made of its content. Moreover, the disputations have turned into tedious sessions in which neither the students nor the teachers place much stock, as evidenced by the first and last rules: "The teacher shall consider the day of disputations no less fruitful and worthy of attention than a day of lecture," and "If there is anything else which is customary to make disputations better attended or more spirited, it shall be carefully preserved" (*Ratio, Common Rules for All Professors of Higher Faculties*, in Fitzpatrick, pp. 154-155).

The use of spies and "black marks" are indications that Latin had failed to be established as the *lingua franca* of the school community. Latin was not used as the medium of instruction. Students' use of spoken Latin was limited to the recitation of grammar rules and the repetition of memorized phrases.

It is possible that students not only did not want to speak Latin, they could-n't. Two passages in the *Ratio* are telling with regard to the lack of speaking ability among students. First, now that the first three years are spent study-ing rules, rather than using the language to interpret and express meaning, the course in rhetoric becomes essential. The directive is given that students must spend at least one, preferable two, or even three years in rhetoric before they will be admitted to advanced study in philosophy. Parents must have questioned why it was necessary for their children to spend yet another year studying Latin, after they had done little else for three years already, because the *Ratio* states that parents must be convinced of the utility of this extra year: "the necessity of this must be made evident to their parents" (*Ratio, Rules for the Rector,* in Fitzpatrick, p. 140). Second, rhetoric is the only course that does not have a strict examination policy. This is due to the fact that "the grade of this class cannot be easily assigned to certain definite ends: for it instructs to perfect eloquence" (*Ratio, Rules for the Professors of Rhetoric,* in Fitzpatrick, p. 208). However, while in class students must memorize and perform orations. Little practice in extemporaneous speech occurs. Nevertheless, for the first time in the rhetoric class, the directives include explicit reference to students' composition of original texts in addition to the imitation of classical authors.

ERROR CORRECTION

Despite all the difficulty surrounding Latin as a means of oral expression, the Jesuit system retained its emphasis on the development of written fluency. In the grammar courses, writing was limited to dictation in Latin followed by translation into the vernacular and retranslation into Latin. A comparison of the original Latin and the students' final version provided corrective feed-back. Nonetheless, Ignatius's insistence that teachers correct students' "com-positions" found its way into the *Ratio.* Teachers are exhorted to correct at least some of the students' written work, daily when possible. They are instructed that "the general method of correcting papers is as follows: To show if anything is in contradiction to the precepts; to ask how it may be cor-rected; to order the rivals [other students] to correct a mistake publicly as soon as they see it, and to state the precept which was violated; finally to praise anything which is nearly perfect" (*Ratio, Rules Common to the Professors of the Lower Classes,* in Fitzpatrick, pp. 199-200).

Ignatius is vociferous in his views on second language writing, "for what appears in writing needs a closer scrutiny that what is merely spoken, the written word remaining as a perpetual witness which cannot be amended or explained away as easily as is done in talk" (*Letter to Peter Faber,* 1542, in Young, p. 63). In a time when the printing press makes doc-uments available to wide audiences, the distinction between private and public correspondence is judiciously guarded. Ignatius is careful to distin-guish formal from informal writing and counseled the members of the

Order to pay careful attention in the organization and content of any letters destined for public consumption. Such "principal" letters, once written, should be reread, corrected, and rewritten before being sent, unlike the "separate sheets" that could be attached for the more personal news that "one may write hurriedly out of the abundance of the heart, with or without a predetermined order" (in Young, p. 63). Furthermore, he pays considerable attention to the appropriateness of language, rather than its form, warning his religious peers that their letters should contain "an abundance of ideas rather than of words" (*Letter to Father Robert Clayssone*, 1555, in Young, p. 376).

Only in the context of writing does Ignatius address language correction directly. He states repeatedly that teachers must correct students' written work. He also addresses error correction twice outside the classroom context. In one exchange, Ignatius criticizes the inappropriate content of the correspondence sent by members of the Order. In reply, Father Nicholas Bobadilla points out two errors in Ignatius's own letter, written in the vernacular: first, the use of "expedir" which should have been "expender;" second, the phrase "de los romanos" which, according to Bobadilla, should have been written "de romanos," a mistake which evidently caused some hilarity among its readers. In his response to Bobadilla, Ignatius attributes the first error to faulty transcription that he didn't correct because it wasn't part of the principal, or formal, letter. For the second, Ignatius explains his reasoning in supplying the article, and then acquiesces:

> But if there was a fault in writing "de los romanos," I will say hereafter, "En el corte del rey de romanos. [...] If everybody laughed at that, as you say they did, I should think that, when you saw that some laughed, you would not have shown it to everybody (*Letter to Father Nicholas Bobadilla*, 1543, in Young, p. 74).

In a different letter, responding to the concern that a lack of correction may lead students to believe that they haven't erred, Ignatius replies:

> To the second part of the tenth [question], as to whether one should be left under the false impression that there is no imperfection, [...] it might be better for the person's progress to do so; that the more one attends to the faults of others, the less he will see of his own, and thus make no progress himself (*Letter to Father Anthony Brandao*, 1551, in Young, p. 242).

Given his insistence that all should come to learn Latin "according to their ability" (*Letter to Father John Pelletier*, 1551, in Young, p. 247), the recognition that "in humane letters and in languages no time limit for passing through courses can be prescribed because of the variation in the talents and in the learning of the students" (*Constitutions*, Part IV, Chapter 15, in Fitzpatrick 1933, p. 108), and the sensitive response to correction detailed above, it is difficult to accept that the myriad of rules regarding accuracy of form and correction of grammar as stated in the *Ratio* reflect the spirit of Ignatius's views on the subject of linguistic errors.

The discipline of the Jesuit system is well-established; whereas Ignatius's own writings stress moral obedience, the *Ratio* insists on correction. Numerous pages are devoted to who is to be reprimanded for which offense, by whom, in what manner, and ranging from correction of compositions and examinations to the correction of moral defects. Perhaps it is only to be expected that a system based on rules would emphasize the consequences of transgression.

CONCLUSION

The authors of the *Ratio* were clearly familiar with the day-to-day problems facing teachers and school administrators. They provided, to the last detail, the answer to the question: "What should I do on Monday?" They specified the responsibilities of everyone from the rector to the janitor. The last sections of the document stipulate the rules regarding defacement of school property. They also speak in the strongest of terms against students carrying weapons to school. However, in their zeal to prescribe solutions to every imaginable problem that may arise, they lost Ignatius's vision. Latin was no longer a functional language in the Jesuit college and, therefore, students failed to acquire functional language ability. True, students practiced translation. Text remained important for the information it contained, but it was no longer the vehicle for language learning. Surely, the failure of Latin to become the language of wider communication among the general populace played a major role in its demise in the curriculum. But the separation of language and content had far-reaching and lasting effects on language teaching.

The trend toward rules, prevalent in all aspects of sixteenth-century life, overpowered the humanist theory of language teaching supported by Ignatius and Guarino. Scaglione (1986) suggests that "the normative, deductive method based on learned rules enjoyed a sort of revival in the authoritarian climate brought about by the struggles for and against the Reformation" (p. 10). However, despite the hiatus of a century, a striking similarity exists between the *Ratio* and Battista's treatise, on the one hand, and the beliefs shared by Ignatius and Guarino on the other. The discrepancy between the theoretical tradition and the handbooks for language teachers remains to be explained.

It could be argued that in any translation from theory into practice, something of the underlying theory is lost. For both Guarino da Verona and Ignatius of Loyola, others' interpretations of their writing—albeit similar in scope and treatment and sometimes containing verbatim excerpts from the original works—diverge considerably from the original ideas about language learning and teaching. Furthermore, the deviation is in the same direction.

The last historical case, Comenius, will show that such distortions are not restricted to second-party interpretations of one's writing. They can arise from the original author as he attempts to institutionalize his own ideas.

P_ause to consider . . ._

why the teaching of rules has such great appeal for many language teachers, even when they know that the explicit knowledge of a rule does not ensure that a learner will be able to apply it during spontaneous language use. What impact may a change in emphasis from knowledge of rules to the ability to use the language in a variety of contexts have on the way students' language development is assessed?

CHAPTER THREE

The Textbook Writer: Institutionalization and the Curriculum

Johannes Amos Comenius (1592–1670)

Languages are easier to learn by practice than from rules.
—Johannes Amos Comenius,
The Great Didactic, 1657, Rule 3, p. 206

But rules assist and strengthen the knowledge derived from practice.
—Johannes Amos Comenius,
The Great Didactic, Rule 4, p. 206

On their way to making Latin the language of world-wide communication, the humanists missed the boat. Despite the fact that in Guarino's time Latin had all the potential—a rich literary tradition, cultural prestige, official status in government and diplomacy, in fact, very much like English has today—it could not assume such a role. The presence of too many co-existent factors contributed to its demise. A political climate in which nationalistic objectives were paramount was at odds with the promotion of a means for international communication. The intense religious hatred, which erupted across the continent (not only between Roman Catholics and Protestants, but within the groups themselves), could never have supported a world language that was at once identified with the Roman church and representative of a pagan culture. The once dominant Catholic Spain, already in deterioration during the latter part of the fifteenth century, succumbed to the increasing economic power of France, Holland, and England. Fierce religious antagonism, international wars, and economic imbalance characterized a confused and violent Europe in the seventeenth century.

Intellectual life on the continent offered no oasis from the chaos as scientists, such as Galileo Galilei, Johannes Kepler, and Anton van Leeuwenhoek, challenged long-standing beliefs rooted in Aristotelian physics. With evidence obtained through the use of the telescope, Galileo confirmed Copernicus's hypothesis that the universe is heliocentric, not geocentric: In doing so, he inflamed Church authorities and was tried for heresy. Kepler discovered the elliptical orbits of the planets around the sun. At the opposite physical extreme, van Leeuwenhoek's use of homemade lenses permitted the investigation of microscopic entities (i.e., bacteria, protozoa, and other microorganisms), thus providing visual proof to confirm William Harvey's theory of the circulation of red blood cells.

The effects of the new science of observation and experimentation reverberated throughout the intellectual community as the validity of the ancient authors' authority was called into question. The dependence on ecclesiastical authority and Latin as an intermediary language had already been obviated in the religious realm. Individuals now interpreted Scripture for themselves in their mother tongues, thanks to the proliferation of translations of the Bible (Luther's German translation of the New Testament in 1522 and the Old Testament in 1534; English translation by Tyndale in 1526 and authorized King James version in 1611; Czech edition in 1568; Welsh edition in 1588; and London Polyglot Bible—in ten languages—in 1653). In the scientific sphere, the ability of an individual to understand phenomena by virtue of one's senses, through the power of keen observation, undermined a reliance on suspect secondary sources like the classical authors.

Ironically, one of the major factors in the decline of Latin may also have been in the language teaching methods of the schools themselves. Rather than bolster the status of Latin, an emphasis on translation and the use of the mother tongue may have served to accelerate its extinction. Although the study of Latin continued to dominate the curriculum, it was no longer the medium of instruction. The vernacular had become the language of class-rooms and of textbooks. New books employing a technique known as inter-linear translation appeared on the market. In these texts, Latin passages and their vernacular equivalents existed side by side or in alternating lines, a print version of the "subtitled" lectures recommended by the Jesuit *Ratio*. Not only did students not need to speak Latin in class, they did not need to be able to read it either. Because Latin no longer had a communicative purpose, students failed to acquire functional proficiency in Latin. If Latin had been established as the *lingua franca* of instruction, it might have maintained some functional role, at least as the language of education, instead of lapsing fur-ther into pedanticism and artifact. Nonetheless, the educational system of the sixteenth century had not yet entirely abandoned the teaching of Latin. Even though it neither served the society at large nor the more intimate classroom community, Latin retained its position as an arcane subject in the school cur-riculum.

Despite the efforts of the humanists, Latin could not maintain its status as the language of wider communication. It remained the intellectual prop-erty of a dwindling elite and, in doing so, it was eventually vanquished by the vernacular languages. Already in the previous century, perceptive and practical Ignatius saw this possibility, but could do nothing to stop it. In the Protestant schools of the seventeenth century, the goal of acquiring commu-nicative ability in Latin was dealt its final blow.

JOHANNES AMOS COMENIUS: A LIFETIME OF TEXTBOOKS

Johannes Amos Comenius's vision for educational reform was on an even grander scale than that of either Guarino or Ignatius of Loyola. Throughout his long and arduous career, he outlined curricula from infancy through the university, advocated a universal system of education, and proposed the invention of a new world language to replace Latin, which by the mid-seventeenth century had been supplanted by the vernacular for anything other than law or the most scholarly pursuits. Comenius was famous in his time, however, not for his many philosophical and theological treatises, but for his textbooks, the *Janua Linguarum Reserata* (*The Gate of Tongues, Unlocked*) in 1631, the *Vestibulum* (*The Vestibule*) in 1633, and the *Orbis Sensualium Pictus* (*The World of Things in Pictures*) in 1658. One may argue that Comenius's con-tribution to Western education simply exploited the printing press, which afforded the possibility of creating standard editions of textbooks accessible to all students. The success of his textbooks, however, appeared to mark a dramatic shift in language teaching. Who was this man whose language text-books were so popular that they continued to be published throughout Europe for almost 200 years after his death?

He was born Jan Amos Komensky on March 28, 1592, in the small town of Nivnitz in Moravia (a region of central Europe in the present-day Czech Republic). The son of prosperous mill owners, his life of misfortune began when he was orphaned at around age 11 and cheated out of the family inheritance by his guardians. According to a biographer, Comenius's early attendance at the elementary school at the opposite end of the valley in the city of Strasnitz was "unproductive" (Keatinge 1910). According to Comenius himself, the two years he spent at the Latin school well north of Strasnitz in the town of Prerau (Prerov) were useless:

> I remember well that, when we began to learn dialectic, rhetoric, and metaphysics, we were, at the very beginning, overburdened with long-winded rules, with commentaries and notes on commentaries, with comparisons of authors and with knotty questions. Latin grammar was taught us with all the exceptions and irregularities; Greek grammar with all its dialects, and we, poor wretches, were so confused that we scarcely understood what it was all about (*The Great Didactic*, Chapter 16, 1657, p. 122).

In reality, his experiences in the elementary and Latin schools in Moravia were far from futile: they provided the motivation for his career as a major proponent of educational reform.

Comenius revolted against what he perceived as the tremendous inefficiency of the schools, referring to them as places where thousands of poor wretches like himself "miserably lost the sweetest spring-time of their whole life, and have wasted the fresh years of youth" (pp. 79-80). In his writings, he laid most of the blame for this appalling situation on the methods employed, arguing that all children can be educated and that, when they are not, the fault lies with the teacher for not knowing how to teach them.

Comenius's ultimate pedagogical goal, however, entailed more than just curricular or methodologic reform. Like Guarino and Ignatius before him, he was an intensely religious man whose educational mission possessed a strong moral component. He proposed a tripartite system of education: one that would confer knowledge, morality, and piety. Whereas the humanists had reconciled their Christian beliefs with the *studia humanitatis*, Comenius's religious convictions—in combination with a revised scientific paradigm— forced a reevaluation of the importance of the classical authors in the curriculum. The tension and contradictions between Comenius's religious beliefs and the humanist curriculum, as well as the intellectual turmoil resulting from a rapidly shifting paradigm for science in seventeenth-century Europe, are reflected in the pedagogical works of a man who sought harmony at all costs.

Like his father, Comenius was a member of the Moravian Protestant church also known as the "Church of the Brethren" or "Unitas Fratrum." Formed in 1457, this sect followed the teachings of Jan Hus and believed in simple worship accompanied by strict Christian living, relying on the Bible as the rule of faith. In preparation for ordination as a minister in the sect, Comenius matriculated at the university at Herborn in Nassau (in present Germany) at age 18. While there, he studied educational methods and read an essay by Wolfgang Ratke on the reformation of schools in Germany. Upon completion of his studies, he traveled throughout northern Europe before returning on foot to his native Moravia in 1614.

Because he was only 22 at the time and could not seek ordination until he was 24, Comenius assumed the management of a Moravian school at Prerau. The experience marked his first attempt to teach Latin to schoolboys and the beginning of his quest to outline an easier way to do it. Once he was ordained a minister, Comenius became pastor and school inspector in Fulnek, a town to the northeast and just a few valleys distant from Prerau. For the next three decades, the Roman Catholic Church, aided especially by the Jesuits, relentlessly persecuted non-Catholics. This historical context affected in myriad ways the personal and professional life of this man who combined, with equal fervor, the roles of evangelical minister and educational reformer. When the chief Bohemian Protestant was executed in Prague, in June, 1621, Comenius's religious exile began. The city of Fulnek was plundered and burned by the Spanish, and he lost all his worldly possessions: his home, his entire library, and his manuscripts. The following year his wife and children died in an epidemic.

Two years later, Comenius remarried, this time the daughter of a Moravian pastor who brought with her a small fortune. But shortly afterward, an order was issued for all non-Catholic preachers and pastors to leave Bohemia and Moravia. Comenius, thus, went to Poland to investigate the possibility of resettlement there, but in less than a year he returned to Moravia where he lived for two years with his religious community hiding in a forest. Despite adverse circumstances, his interest in school reform, fueled by his religious ideology, never dimmed. In 1627, at the request of a colleague, he drew up some guidelines for teaching. We know from his biographer, Keatinge, that Comenius had read the *Didactic* of the Jesuit Elias Bodinus, as well as the *Janua linguarum* of another Jesuit, William Bath. Clearly, he decided to prepare something similar in his own language. From his own critical assessment of it, it is obvious that he was also familiar with a work entitled *Thesaurum Polono-Latino-Graecum* (*A Thesaurus of Polish, Latin, and Greek*) of Gregory Cnapius, a Polish Jesuit. Although Keatinge dismissed the influence that these specific works had on Comenius—other than the borrowing of their titles for his own publications—in both general and particular ways, the Jesuit educational model influenced much of the substance of his reform.

Throughout his life, Comenius fervently believed that the day would come when the Brethren would be reestablished in Moravia and he would return to reorganize their schools. His dream was interrupted when, in 1628, all evangelicals were expelled from Bohemia by edict. Comenius and his wife went to Lissa, Poland. Under the protection of a Count Raphael, they remained there for 12 years. While in Lissa, Comenius taught at the gymnasium, eventually becoming its rector in 1636. During this time, he gained practical experience as a teacher and administrator. It was during this period that Comenius composed most of the pedagogical works that made him famous.

THE FAULT OF THE SCHOOLS

Schools, Comenius argues, fail in two ways: first, because they do not have suitable teaching materials and, second, "because even in school books the natural order, that the matter come first and the form follow, is not observed. Everywhere the exact opposite is to be found" (*The Great Didactic*, Chapter 16, p. 115). The major culprit is that students are forced to study languages (chiefly Latin, but also Greek) before they are allowed to study anything else: "Languages are learned in schools before the sciences, since the intellect is detained for some years over the study of languages, and only then allowed to proceed to the sciences, mathematics, physics, etc." (p. 115). In Comenius's opinion, this is a grave error because, for language learning to occur, instruction in language must be accompanied by instruction in things: "Things are essential, words only accidental. (...) Both should therefore be presented to the intellect at the same time, but particularly the things, since they are as much objects of the understanding as are languages" (p. 115).

Another flaw in contemporary pedagogy in Comenius's view lay in the sequence of language instruction itself:

> Even in the study of languages the proper order is reversed, since the students commence, not with some author or with a skilfully compiled phrase book, but with the grammar; though authors (and in their own way the phrase books) present the material of speech, namely words, while the grammars, on the other hand, only give the form, that is to say, the laws of the formation, order and combination of words (pp. 115-116).

The remedy for this situation is to combine content and language in the curriculum: "Instruction in language must go hand in hand with instruction in facts" (p. 177). To reverse this "natural order" by the presentation of rules first only ensures that students will be totally confused:

> Beginners in grammar are so overwhelmed by precepts, rules, exceptions to the rules, and exceptions to the exceptions, that for the most part they do not know what they are doing, and are quite stupefied before they begin to understand anything (p. 196).

The practice of teaching rules, followed by a few examples, contradicts the natural order. Comenius believes that students derive more benefit from examples than from precepts: "It is the abstract rules that are first taught and then illustrated by dragging in a few examples; though it is plain that a light should precede him whom it lights" (p. 116).

The Remedy: Materials

Comenius corrects these perceived pedagogical flaws by providing teaching materials that are at once age appropriate and pedagogically sound: in which things are taught first, followed by how to express those things in language. His methodology ensures the following three principles: "that no language be learned from a grammar, but from suitable authors," "that the understanding be first instructed in things, and then taught to express them in language," and "that examples come before rules" (p. 116).

Based on his belief that materials play an essential role in school reform, Comenius composes a series of textbooks whose content and structure, he argues, are more appropriate for schoolboys than are the works of classical authors. In 1631, Comenius publishes the *Janua Linguarum Reserata*, a volume that contains 8,000 of the most common Latin words arranged to form 1,000 sentences. The text progresses from short, simple sentences in the early chapters to gradually more syntactically complex constructions. In keeping with the notion that knowledge of everyday phenomena is eminently more practical for beginners than is the study of Cicero, each of the 100 chapters deals with one class of phenomena (e.g., fire, diseases, trade, arithmetic, and angels). This was done to introduce students to language and content simultaneously, in accordance with the *Janua*'s basic tenet that thought and language should proceed together.

The success of the *Janua* was "extraordinary" (Keatinge 1910, p. 23), as evidenced by its eventual "translation"—for the Latin sentences and their vernacular equivalents both appeared in the text—into twelve European languages and several Asian ones as well. The inclusion of the vernacular translations of the Latin sentences reflects Comenius's belief that the study of Latin requires the mediation of the mother tongue. This point is discussed again later in reference to his theory of language learning (p.45 ff).

Critics of the work expressed disbelief that students learned Latin any better with the *Janua* than they did with older methods, and they ridiculed the style and inaccuracy of the Latin itself. A German, Adelung, later remarked that universal use of the *Janua* would have been the surest way of restoring the barbarous Latin of the Middle Ages ("*Die Barbarey der mittleren Zeiten*," quoted in Keatinge, p. 24). However, if we are to believe its success—the many editions that were circulated and the renown that it brought to its author—teachers must have loved it. Perhaps anything would have been an improvement over what was happening in schools at the time. If teachers were dissatisfied with the results of their instruction, they might have been anxious to adopt textbooks that appeared to be more "suitable" for young people and that claimed to make the process of learning Latin "easier."

Notwithstanding Comenius's attempt to make the *Janua* accessible to beginning students, his method must not have been as explicit within the text as he had believed. Teachers complained that the *Janua* was too difficult for their students. Although we do not know precisely the nature of the difficulty encountered, we do know that Comenius quickly responded to their need with an even more simplified text, the *Vestibulum*. This book, preparatory to the *Janua*, consists of 1,000 of the most common Latin words arranged into 427 simple sentences, as the following examples from the first chapter illustrate:

> De accidentibus rerum
> Deus est aeternus, mundus temporarius.
> Angelus immortalis, homo mortalis.
> Corpus visibile, spiritus invisibilis, anima itidem.
> Coelum est supremum, Aer medius, Terra infima.
> (About the rudiments of things
> God is eternal, the world temporary.
> Angels are immortal, humans mortal.
> The body is visible, the spirit invisible, the soul likewise.
> Heaven is highest, air is in the middle, Earth is lowest.)

In subsequent editions of the *Vestibulum,* Comenius reduces the simple sentences still further, arriving eventually at Latin-vernacular word lists. The revisions of the *Vestibulum* suggest an order of presentation in conflict with Comenius's original intent. In one of many contradictory statements, he argues that before students confront facts they must study first the lexicon, then the grammar of a language:

> First, rising from its roots, comes the forest of Latin words, the lexicon. Then we give you the tools for cutting this forest down, sawing the trees into planks and fastening these together, namely, the grammar. Finally we place before you a short universal history of objects, fashioned out of all the words in Latin properly fitted together, namely, the text of the *Janua* (*The Great Didactic*, Chapter 10, p. 74).

Seen through his textbook revisions, Comenius appears to have reversed his ideas on the order of instruction, now suggesting that, instead of language and facts progressing hand in hand, students must master the grammar before they are introduced to content. The incongruence between the original theory of language learning and the directions for teaching practice parallels Comenius's struggle to reconcile conflicting religious beliefs and to straddle scientific paradigms.

In 1635, with his fame spreading in tandem with his textbooks, Comenius was asked to prepare some guidelines for the reorganization of the gymnasium at Breslau (Wroclaw, a city in Silesia, now in southwestern Poland). He wrote the *De sermonis Latini studio dissertatio (Dissertation on the Study of the Latin Language)* in which he once again stresses the importance of acquiring a knowledge of facts over a mere accumulation of words. Learning words without fully understanding the meaning behind them, Comenius writes, is just "words without referents, thoughts without substance, a sheath without a sword, a shadow without a body, a body without a soul" (*De Sermonis Latini Studio Dissertatio* in *Opera Didactica Magna*, p. 348, translation mine). Paradoxically, the evolution of Comenius's textbooks evokes the same loss of substance, with a progressive reduction of language from the paragraph-level discourse of the *Janua* to the sentences and, in later editions, wordlists of the *Vestibulum*.

Materials play a major part in Comenius's reform. The organization of the schools and even the division of the classes within them are structured on the "specially prepared" textbooks they are to adopt (*The Great Didactic*, Chapter 29, p. 269). All children enter the Vernacular School at age seven. The curriculum of the six grades of the school is based on six textbooks, books whose titles Comenius proposes, but which apparently are never published. Next, students attend the Latin School for another six years. The first two classes of this school use the *Vestibulum* for the first six months, and the *Janua* for the remaining year and a half. The third-year class studies the *Palatium* (*The Palace*), a collection of letters and dialogs created out of phrases adapted from the classical authors. The fourth-year class reads the *Thesaurus*, carefully selected excerpts from the classical authors. Such passages repeat subjects already dealt with in the *Janua* and thus serve as a kind of expanded review. This curriculum, however, could not have been realized as the *Vestibulum* and the *Janua* were his only textbooks in print at the time.

Still, Comenius's renown as a textbook author increased. In 1638, he was invited to Sweden to participate in the reform of their schools. Although he refused the invitation, its issuance must have caused Comenius to realize that schools throughout the European continent were in need of reform. Thus, he began to translate his manuscript on methodology, *Didactica Magna* (*The Great Didactic*) from the original Czech into Latin so that it might reach a larger audience. The Latin version did not appear in print, however, until 1657.

His textbooks, not his methodology, were Comenius's claim to international fame. The *Janua* had been well received in England. In 1641, a friend of Milton hinted that he might find Comenius some financial aid in England to facilitate his work. Comenius was excited by this possibility because what he really wanted to compose was not more textbooks, but an encyclopedia of knowledge, his *Pansophia* (*Universal Knowledge*). The goal of education within the philosophy of pansophism is a universal knowledge shared by all people and all nations. Never convinced that Latin and the classics need form the core of the curriculum, Comenius was more interested in exploring alternative educational schemes than in promoting Latin. Buoyed by the idea that the English government would provide financial support for such an endeavor, he quit his post at Lissa and set off for England.

Upon arrival, Comenius joined a circle of intellectual friends who sought to develop a universal college for the study of physical phenomena. One of the interesting goals of this endeavor was the establishment of a universal language. Comenius first opposed the suggestion that Latin could serve such a purpose, maintaining that it was "too difficult." He proposed that a new tongue be invented, one that would be easier and more complete than any existing language. Although this and other interesting ideas were bandied about, in the course of the year no government funds were forthcoming. Without financial support, it was clear that Comenius could not remain in England.

Comenius also could not return to Lissa, having quit his position; he was in need of a new patron. He found one, a successful Dutch merchant, de Geer. Even though his business office was in Amsterdam, de Geer lived in Sweden and, thus, Comenius's former Swedish connection was reestablished. Under the delusion that he was to pursue his pansophic writings, Comenius accepted de Geer's offer. In truth, however, de Geer wanted textbooks for the reformed schools of Sweden. Comenius resigned himself to working on what he now referred to as his spinosa didactica (thorny methodology) for a couple of years—just for the money—so that he could return to his pansophic project. The "couple of years" turned out to be six long and frustrating years for a man whose heart was no longer in textbook writing or methodology.

In 1642, Comenius settled in the seaport town of Elbing (Elblag) in northern Poland to begin another revision of the *Janua*, along with a lexicon and grammar to accompany it, for Swedish schoolboys. Continually distracted by religious and philosophical meanderings, he finally dispatched some books to Sweden in 1647. Then Comenius was elected senior bishop of the Moravian Brethren and was recalled to Lissa. On the way, his wife died.

Comenius's return to Lissa coincided with the end of the religious struggles and series of battles for European power known as the Thirty Years' War. Unfortunately, the Treaty of Westphalia failed to bring the political and religious harmony that Comenius had long anticipated. Religious tolerance was extended to the Calvinists and Lutherans, but not to the Brethren. Comenius's life goal—to reform the schools of Moravia—would not be realized. Meanwhile, he married for a third time. In 1650, he went, by invitation, to Saros-Patak, in Hungary, to begin a universal school based on his pansophic ideas.

At about the same time, Comenius began to sketch out yet another textbook, the *Orbis Sensualium Pictus* (*The World of Things in Pictures*), a text intended for children in the "Mother School," (i.e., the years spent at the mother's knee prior to enrolling in the Vernacular, or elementary, School, in Comenius's plan for education). The success of the *Orbis Sensualium Pictus* was "even more extraordinary" than that of the *Janua*. The *Orbis Pictus*— along with the Bible—formed an essential part of the home library for generations of children (Keatinge 1910, p. 78).

		About the walls, and the Gates,	Circa Mænia, & Portas,
		are the Magazine, 9.	Armamentarium, 9.
		the Granary, 10.	Granarium, 10.
		Innes,	Diverforia,
		Ale-houfes,	Popinæ,
		Cooks-fhops, 11	& Caupona, 11.
		the Play-houfe, 12.	Theatrum, 12.
		and the Spittle; 13.	Nofodochium; 13.
		In the by-places	· In receffibus,
		are houfes of office,14.	Forica (Cloacæ) 14.
		and the Prifon. 15.	& Cuftodia(Carcer)15.
		In the chief Steeple	In Turre primariâ
		is the Clock, 16.	eft Horologium, 16.
Within a City	Intra Urbem	and the Watchmens	& habitacio
are Streets, 1.	funt Platea (Vici) 1.	dwelling. 17.	Vigilum. 17.
paued with Stones;	lapidibus ftratæ:	In the Streets	In Plateis
Market-places, 2.	Fora, 2.	are Wells. 18.	funt Putei. 18.
(In fome places	(alicubi	The River 19.	Fluvius, 19.
with Galleries) 3.	cum Porticibus) 3.	or Beck	vel Rivus,
and narrow Lanes, 4.	& Angiportis. ᵪ.	runing about the City,	Urbem interfluens,
The publick buildings	Publica ædificia funt	ferueth	infervit
are in the middle of the	in medio Urbis,	to wash away the filth.	fordibus eluendis.
the Church, 5. (City,	Templum, 5.	The Tower 10.	Arx 20.
the School, 6.	Schola, 6.	ftandeth in the higheft	exftat
the Guild-hall, 7.	Curia, 7.	part of the City.	in fummo Urbis.
the Exchange. 8.	Domus Mercaturæ: 8.		

The inward parts of a city / Interiora Urbis in J. A. Comenius *Orbis Sensualium pictus*.

In fact, the *Orbis Pictus* constitutes a true breakthrough in educational practice. Scholars acknowledge its importance as the first picture book for children. As a pedagogical device, it was meant to teach the vocabulary of real-world objects and events. It is unique in its interdependence of illustrations and text: The pictures in the *Orbis Pictus* are not supplemental; they constitute an essential part of the text itself. This combination represents a radical departure from earlier uses of illustrations as mere decorations or as devices to help the reader visualize mythical or figurative passages in the text.

Unfortunately for Comenius, the success of the *Orbis Pictus* was not mirrored in the school reorganization plan at Saros-Patak. Having failed to implement the reforms that he wanted—it seems the teachers were not very cooperative—Comenius again returned to Lissa just in time to see it sacked by invaders. Once again, he lost his entire library, including all of his research on pansophia. Comenius returned to Amsterdam at the request of de Geer's son, Laurence, who agreed to continue his father's patronage. In 1657, the younger de Geer subsidized the publication of a 1,000-page folio of Comenius's works: *J. A. Comenii Opera Omnia Didactica* (*The Complete Didactic Works of J.A. Comenius*). The last thirteen years of Comenius's life were spent in religious and metaphysical pursuits. He died in Amsterdam on November 15, 1670. His educational legacy is preserved in the 1657 folio. It contains all of Comenius's pedagogical works, including copies of his textbooks, along with a little-known methods book, the *Didactica Magna* (*The Great Didactic*) that was dwarfed in comparison.

***P**ause to consider . . .*

that until the widespread use of the printing press, teachers could not rely on the availability of standardized texts: Students who had any books may have had different editions, varying translations, or inaccurate copies. How important are standardized materials in language teaching today? Do they supplement the curriculum, or define it?

THE GREAT DIDACTIC, *OR THE ART OF TEACHING*

As significant as Comenius believed good materials were to successful school reform, they were not nearly as important as he believed methodology to be. The *Didactica Magna* is testimony to this belief. Composed between 1628 and 1632 during his stay in Lissa, it describes Comenius's ideas on education in general and language teaching in particular. Although an examination of this treatise reveals numerous discrepancies and contradictions in Comenius's theory of second language learning and recommendations for teaching practice, the one issue on which he never wavers is his absolute confidence in the power of method.

At the beginning of the volume, Comenius states with absolute confidence that adherence to his method ensures 100% effective, pleasant, and thorough instruction in both academics and morals:

> We venture to promise a GREAT DIDACTIC, that is to say, the whole art of teaching all things to all men, and indeed of teaching them with certainty, so that the result cannot fail to follow; further, of teaching them pleasantly, that is to say, without annoyance or aversion on the part of teacher or pupil, but rather with the greatest enjoyment for both; further of teaching them thoroughly, not superficially and showily, but in such a manner as to lead to true knowledge, to gentle morals, and to the deepest piety (*The Great Didactic*, "Greeting to the Reader," p. 5).

The reader is assured not only that students will learn, but that they will do so in the most delightful way, without sacrificing academic rigor; in addition, they will exit from the process in possession of the highest virtues. The moral component of Comenius's plan was central, "especially at the present time and in the present condition of morals, when they have sunk so low that, as Cicero says, all should join to bridle them and keep them in check" (p. 6).

Lest one fear finding in the treatise a simple rehash of existent methods, Comenius assures that his methodology is indeed new and improved: "This art of teaching and of learning was in former centuries to a great extent unknown, at any rate in that degree of perfection to which it is now wished to raise it." It is also, he claims, almost entirely of his own invention. He admits that, although he tried to enlist the aid of others in its preparation, all refused: "Putting on one side the discoveries, thoughts, observations, and admonitions of others, I began myself to investigate the matter thoughtfully and to seek out the causes, the principles, the methods, and the objects of the art of teaching" (p. 8-9).

A preliminary chapter of the book, entitled "Use of the Art of Teaching," describes the advantages that the method provides to parents, teachers, students, schools, states, the church, and God. Parents benefit because they can be assured that their children will learn under this system: "Now that the method of teaching has been reasoned out with unerring accuracy, it will, with the assistance of God, be impossible that the desired result should not follow" (p. 19). Through the use of this method, parents save time and money: They no longer need to hire tutors for their children, bribe them, or cajole them to study (p. 19). Teachers save time and energy: They needn't try "in turn one plan then another" because they possess the one method to follow (p. 19). Students certainly gain because they master the sciences "without difficulty, tedium, complaints, or blows, as if in sport and in merriment" as well as reach their maximum potential "on account of the infallibility of the method" (p. 19).

The benefits of Comenius's method transcend the sphere of the individual: They permeate society. The positive results obtained would undoubtedly create an increase in demand for education. The number of schools, in turn, will multiply, accommodating more and more students. Thus, nations will benefit from such mass education of youth, because they are "the foundation of the whole state" (p. 20). Most importantly for the Moravian bishop, the kingdom of God will flourish because the word will reach more people and have more influence when it is taught in the schools, and because educated minds will be more receptive to it than ignorant ones (p. 20-21).

After such an arrogant start, the modern reader may be surprised by Comenius's statement, in a decidedly meeker tone, that he is simply fulfilling his Christian duty to share his methodology, his "divine gift," with others. He chided his own lack of intellectual stature: "Christian readers, suffer me to speak with you confidentially! My more intimate friends know that I am a man of little ability and almost without literary training" (p. 9). This typically baroque juxtaposition of the two extremes, the boasting, infallible methodologist and the self-deprecating, humble servant, is only the first—but a particularly apt—characterization of Comenius's contradictory nature. It represents his ongoing struggle to straddle opposing paradigms: the humanist and the reformed Christian, Aristotle and the new science. Throughout his pedagogical writings, Comenius is also torn between a theory of language learning that is meaning-driven and a method of language teaching that is form-focused.

Because in Comenius's vision for a new society everyone requires education, every city, town, or village must have a school (p. 76). He reminds the reader that such a recommendation is in direct keeping with Martin Luther's exhortation as expressed in the *Letter to the Mayors and Aldermen of All of Cities of Germany in Behalf of Christian Schools* and the *Sermon on the Duty of Sending Children to School* (in Ulich 1954). He insists that education should not be the prerogative solely of those in privileged positions of authority, but must be extended to include those in subordinate positions as well. In this way, citizens will obey civil authority, not because of force, but because they understand the reason for such control, and they will do so of their own free will and love of order (*The Great Didactic*, Chapter 6, p. 56).

The best time to begin that education is with the very young because they are at their most receptive and because all humanity will benefit. The argument raised in the first pages of the treatise is thus reiterated: "If the corruption of the human race is to be remedied, this must be done by means of the careful education of the young" because "if we wish to have well-ordered and prosperous Churches, states, and households, thus and in no other way can we reach our goal" (*The Great Didactic*, "Dedicatory Letter," pp. 15, 18). To make his case for the schooling of young children, Comenius cites both Scripture and nature: religion and science. He exploits all the classical metaphors: the initial pliancy of wax; the vessel that forever retains the essence of what it first carried; and the sapling that conforms its shape to its early environment. He corroborates these metaphors with those peculiar to his time, taken specifically from the specialization of labor and mass production. He reminds the reader that if you were to need flour, you would go to the miller, shoes to the cobbler, a key to the locksmith. Therefore, for instruction, you would go to school. This is just one of many instances in which Comenius borrows his terms of comparison for the school from the world of the factory or the workshop. The inference is that the teacher supplies the commodity, knowledge, and that the schoolroom is a place in which scholars are manufactured like shoes or keys. In fact, Comenius's method is touted above all for its machine-like efficiency. He proclaims that with the proper method one teacher can instruct many children, hundreds in fact, simultaneously, just like the printing press turns out books. The mass education of children is compared to the cultivation of fruit orchards, or fish hatcheries (pp. 64-65).

---

*P*ause to consider . . .

how the technology of his time greatly influenced Comenius's choice of metaphors to use to describe the learning process. What are the metaphors of our age? To what extent might they determine which aspects of the process are discussed and investigated?

CONFLICT OF POLITICS: AGAINST
THE JESUIT SYSTEM

On the one hand, Comenius's advocacy of mass public education for children can be viewed as obedient acquiescence to Luther's ideology. On the other, however, it also represents a direct challenge to the most highly regarded educational system of the time: that of the Jesuits. Comenius is well aware of the esteem in which Jesuit instruction is held. When he contends that no good schools exist, he does not state it inadvertently. He describes those schools that do exist as riddled with problems, the foremost of which is that they are elitist: "Where schools exist, they are not for the whole community, but only for the rich" (p. 77). Apparently, Ignatius's plea to welcome boys of all economic stations had gone for the most part unheeded. In comparison, Comenius's pedagogical approach sounds very egalitarian. Because he asserts that without education neither wealth nor ornament matters, it isn't surprising that he supports the education of rich and poor alike. But what is significant is that from the start he champions, at length, precisely those students whom the Jesuits ignore: not only the very young and the poor, but even the less academically gifted.

The Jesuit bias toward intellectual talent is infamous. Ignatius himself recommends that even the weakest and most sickly boy be admitted to studies when he shows academic promise, "for such persons may be useful even if they have one foot in the grave" (*Letter to Father Urban Fernandes*, Young, 1959, p. 236). Thus, to make his point against the Jesuits even more forcefully, Comenius contends that even downright stupidity is no excuse for remaining untutored: "Nor can any man be found whose intellect is so weak that it cannot be improved by culture" (*The Great Didactic*, Chapter 9, p. 67). In a bizarre adaptation of a common pedagogical metaphor—the sieve—Comenius proclaims the benefit of instructing the feeble-minded:

> A sieve, if you continually pour water through it, grows cleaner and cleaner, although it cannot retain liquid; and, in the same way, the dull and the weak-minded, though they may make no advance in letters, become softer in disposition and learn to obey the civil magistrates and the ministers of the Church (p. 67).

If we were to follow Comenius's reasoning, education would be advantageous to the witless, not because it would teach them anything, but rather because it would render them inert, more pliable to authority. Furthermore, he reminds the reader that some who may be labeled stupid may merely be late-bloomers. He also argues the power of hard work and effort over innate intelligence. What is particularly daring in the discussion, however, is his statement on the schooling of girls.

Although we find girls among some of the most accomplished pupils under the tutelage of the early Italian humanists, the Jesuit colleges did not admit females. Conversely, Luther himself advocates literacy education for all, boys and girls alike. Comenius appears to wholeheartedly embrace Luther's position and even embellish it in his opening remarks in support of the education of girls:

> Nor can any sufficient reason be given why the weaker sex (to give a word of advice on this point in particular) should be altogether excluded from the pursuit of knowledge (whether in Latin or in their mother-tongue). They also are formed in the image of God, and share in His grace and in the kingdom of the world to come. They are endowed with equal sharpness of mind and capacity for knowledge (often with more than the opposite sex), and they are able to attain the highest positions, since they have often been called by God Himself to rule over nations, to give sound advice to kings and princes, to the study of medicine and of other things which benefit the human race, even to the office of prophesying and of inveighing against priests and bishops. Why, therefore, should we admit them to the alphabet, and afterwards drive them away from books? Do we fear their folly? The more we occupy their thoughts, so much the less will the folly that arises from emptiness of mind find a place (p. 68).

Granted, Comenius believes in some inherent female folly. Nonetheless, he takes the position that women are not only educable but intelligent human beings who can contribute to society in portions equal to and exceeding men. He acknowledges that the same books cannot be given to girls as to boys. What about the biblical and classical invectives against the education of women? Here, Comenius quickly backpedals:

> These opinions, I opine, stand in no true opposition to our demand. For we are not advising that women be educated in such a way that their tendency to curiosity shall be developed, but so that their sincerity and contentedness may be increased, and this chiefly in those things which it becomes a woman to know and to do; that is to say, all that enables her to look after her household and to promote the welfare of her husband and her family (p. 68).

As it turns out, Comenius is not as egalitarian as his earlier statement suggests. Girls may be educated only and precisely in those areas that will make them better wives and mothers.

Comenius must have been aware that the majority would have found even this proposal entirely too radical. He forestalls their reaction with the following:

> If any ask, "What will be the result if artisans, rustics, porters, and even women become lettered?" I answer, If this universal instruction of youth be brought about by the proper means, none of these will lack the material for thinking, choosing, following, and doing good things (p. 69).

"By the proper means," that is, through the use of the correct methodology, "even women" may be educated safely!

In a description of the difference between various schools in his plan, Comenius later states: "The Mother-School and the Vernacular-School embrace all the young of both sexes. The Latin-School gives a more thorough education to those who aspire to higher than the workshop" (p. 258). Clearly "those who aspire" were boys: "Nor should admission to the Latin-School be reserved for the sons of rich men, nobles, and magistrates, as if these were the only boys who would ever be able to fill similar positions" (p. 267). In theory, then, all children—poor, wealthy, bright, dull, male, female—need an elementary education and should, therefore, attend school. Comenius, thus, provides a broad profile of the student population for his reformed schools.

It is not only the Jesuits' undemocratic admissions policy to which Comenius objects; their very pedagogy is flawed:

> Further, the method used in instructing the young has generally been so severe that schools have been looked on as terrors for boys and shambles for their intellects, and the greater number of the students, having contracted a dislike for learning and for books, have hastened away to the workshops of artificers or to some other occupation (p. 77).

According to Comenius's assessment, schools hinder rather than promote learning by the methods they employ.

Those who remained in schools "did not receive a serious or comprehensive education, but a preposterous and wretched one" (p. 77). On what evidence does Comenius base this claim? First and foremost, boys fail to be trained in virtue and piety: "The reason of this evidently is that the question of 'virtuous living' is never raised in the schools" (p. 78). It should be recalled that at this time the Jesuits were under fire for their moral laxity by the puritanical Jansenists, a group formally aligned with the Catholic Church, but which upheld a Calvinistic approach to salvation. In addition to the lack of sound instruction in morals, schools were also rendered ineffective by stifling pedagogical methodology:

> For five, ten, or more years they detained the mind over matters that could be mastered in one. What could have been gently instilled into the intellect, was violently impressed upon it, nay rather stuffed and flogged into it. What might have been placed before the mind plainly and lucidly, was treated of obscurely, perplexedly, and intricately, as if it were a complicated riddle (p. 78).

Precisely, the *studia humanitatis* and Latin are the "matters" that are crammed into youngsters. Comenius explains:

> The study of the Latin language alone (to take this subject as an example), good heavens! How intricate, how complicated, and how

prolix it was! Camp followers and military attendants, engaged in the kitchen and in other menial occupations, learn a tongue that differs from their own, sometimes two or three, quicker than the children in schools learn Latin only, though children have an abundance of time, and devote all their energies to it (p. 79).

Not only do children spend an inordinate amount of time studying Latin, the consequence of their efforts is paltry:

And with what unequal progress (compared to the camp followers and military attendants)! The former gabble their languages after a few months, while the latter, after fifteen or twenty years, can only put a few sentences into Latin with the aid of grammars and of dictionaries, and cannot do even this without mistakes and hesitation. Such a disgraceful waste of time and of labour must assuredly arise from a faulty method (p. 79).

Again Comenius appeals to method as the cure-all and end-all for school reform.

Through the provision of his own teaching methodology, contained in the treatise, Comenius states explicitly what his reform promises, "a system of education," such that:

(i) all the young shall be educated (except those to whom God has denied understanding); (ii) and in all those subjects which are able to make a man wise, virtuous, and pious; (iii) that the process of education, being a preparation for life, shall be completed before maturity is reached; (iv) that this education shall be conducted without blows, rigour, or compulsion, as gently and pleasantly as possible, and in the most natural manner; (v) that the education given shall be not false but real, not superficial but thorough; (the student) shall not merely read the opinions of others and grasp their meaning or commit them to memory and repeat them, but shall himself penetrate to the root of things and acquire the habit of genuinely understanding and making use of what he learns; (vi) that this education shall not be laborious but very easy. The class instruction shall last only four hours each day, and shall be conducted in such a manner that one master may teach hundreds of pupils at the same time, with ten times as little trouble as is now expended on the teaching of one (pp. 81-82).

We recognize that much of what Comenius proposes coincides with what is promised by Battista and the *Ratio* before him: an instructional method that is sound, pleasant, and based on strong moral values. What differentiates his program from earlier ones is the conviction that instruction can be delivered *en masse*. Whereas Guarino and the Jesuits are strong advocates of both individualized attention and small class size, Comenius is adamantly opposed to both.

A "universal" method, like the one Comenius proposes, must be a one-size-fits-all—hundreds at a time—all simultaneously. He has already argued that every child should attend school, and now his plan must accommodate all of those children. What is missing so far in this tableau is the description of the teacher who would be able to accomplish such a feat.

---

*P*ause to consider . . .

how mass second language education—one teacher to many students, all of varying abilities and backgrounds—deals with the issue of the developmental nature of language acquisition.

THE TEACHER, IN THEORY

First and foremost, it is the duty of parents to educate their children, but "since human occupations as well as human beings have multiplied, it is rare to find men who have either sufficient knowledge or sufficient leisure to instruct their children" (p. 61). Parents cannot be relied on to act as teachers because, in Comenius's opinion, they are either too ignorant or too busy: "There are few parents who are in the position to teach their children anything good, either because they have themselves never learned anything of the kind, or because their heads are full of other things; and thus education is neglected" (p. 16). Therefore, the state must enlist professional teachers.

Comenius acknowledges (as did Guarino before him) that good teachers are hard to find. He admonishes the rich who have the means to procure the best tutors for the private education of their children, and thus steal them away from the state and the benefit of the many:

> There are also few teachers who can bring good principles home to the young, and when one arises he is snatched up by some man in high position that he may busy himself with his children; the people get little advantage from him. Thus it comes to pass that the rest of the children grow up without the education that they need (p. 17).

However, the teacher in Comenius's system is himself an enigma. The images that represent him range from the solicitous mother bird which gently nurtures its young in the nest (pp. 112, 114, 116, 123, 124, 126) to the inert ink in the printing press that "conveys information from the books to the minds of the listener" (p. 28). With reference to instruction in moral values, the teacher is likened to a horse tamer: "horse tamers keep a horse under absolute control with an iron bit and ensure its obedience before they teach it its paces" (p. 129). In the majority of instances, however, the teacher is the single source of knowledge that is then poured out on the students, like water from a fountain or the rays of the sun (pp. 163, 165, 166, 250).

According to Comenius, it is the duty of the teacher to cultivate the potential for knowledge that all human beings contain within themselves. Because he upholds Aristotle's notion that the child is a *tabula rasa*, the teacher-artisan must accept total blame should a child fail to learn:

> Aristotle compared the mind of man to a blank tablet on which nothing was written, but on which all things could be engraved. And, just as a writer can write or a painter paint whatever he wishes on a bare tablet, if he be not ignorant of his art, thus it is easy for one who is not ignorant of the art of teaching to depict all things on the human mind. If the result be not successful, it is more than certain that this is not the fault of the tablet (unless it have some inherent defect), but arises from ignorance on the part of the writer or painter (p. 44).

The difference, thus, between a successful teacher and a failed one depends upon the proficiency in "the art of teaching," that is to say, in the Comenius method.

With reference to one last metaphor of the teacher—this time as a technician—Comenius asserts that teachers do not create or need to have any say in what they do because effective teachers simply carry out orders:

> Even masters who have no natural aptitude for teaching will be able to use it (my method) with advantage; since they will not have to select their own subject matter and work out their own method, but will only have to take knowledge that has already been suitably arranged and for the teaching of which suitable appliances have been provided, and to pour it into their pupils. An organist can read any piece of music from his notes, though he might not be able to compose it or to sing or play it from memory; and a schoolmaster, in the same way, should be able to teach anything, if he have before his eyes the subject matter and the method by which it should be taught (p. 288).

Comenius believes that, with appropriate directions, anyone can teach. The teacher is subservient to the method:

> The art of teaching, therefore, demands nothing more than the skilful arrangement of time, of the subjects taught, and of the method. As soon as we have succeeded in finding the proper method it will be no harder to teach schoolboys, in any number desired, than with the help of the printing press to cover a thousand sheets daily with the neatest writing, or with Archimedes' machine to move houses, tow-

ers, and immense weights, or to cross the ocean in a ship, and journey to the New World. The whole process, too, will be as free from
friction as is the movement of a clock whose motive power is supplied by weights. It will be as pleasant to see education carried out
on my plan as to look at an automatic machine of this kind, and the
process will be as free from failure as are these mechanical con-
trivances, when skilfully made (pp. 96-97).

Given the infallibility of the methodology, what necessarily follows is the
automatization of teaching and the mechanization of the teacher.

Earlier Comenius had bemoaned the fact that teachers do not understand their art. He considered that lack of understanding to be one of the
major obstacles to effective instruction. It may seem strange that he apparently does nothing to rectify that situation, especially given the impact of
methodology on an instructor's success. He believes that the materials
themselves dictate the method to such an extent that teachers have no
choice but to implement them. Therefore, no inherent need for theory exists
in their preparation. In fact, teachers are conspicuously absent in the greet-
ing of the "Dedicatory Letter" in *The Great Didactic*: "To all superiors of
human society, to the rulers of states, the pastors of Churches, the parents
and guardians of children, grace and peace from God..." (p. 11). *The Great
Didactic*, the infallible teaching method that Comenius prescribes, is directed
toward persons in positions of authority: heads of state, pastors, and parents. It is not even intended for teachers: The textbooks are sufficient for
their needs.

Comenius proposes the instruction of vast numbers of children under
one teacher and one method because he views students as identical *tabulae
rasae*, like loaves of bread in the bakery or—in a revealing contemporary
metaphor—sheets of paper in the printing press (p. 165). In doing so, he cannot reconcile individual differences within his theory of teaching and learning. He claims that the method works for everyone, and then he quietly rules
out "defective" individuals: those who have not been given the gift of intellect (p. 287) and those who refuse to use it (p. 254). The fifth point in Comenius's plan, however, sounds a note of alarm for the humanists:

That the education given shall be not false but real, not superficial
but thorough; (the student) shall not merely read the opinions of others and grasp their meaning or commit them to memory and repeat
them, but shall himself penetrate to the root of things and acquire the
habit of genuinely understanding and making use of what he learns
(p. 82).

Comenius uses this shift, from "merely reading the opinions of others" to a
personal examination of physical evidence, to redefine the content of a
youth's education.

*P*ause to consider . . .

that Guarino refers to himself in the role of teacher as a loving parent and guide. Ignatius envisions the teacher as someone who knows the intimate details of each student's intellectual development and who can stimulate them to attain their utmost potential. Both reformers take a largely learner-centered approach to language teaching: They see students as active seekers of knowledge, not only eager, but influential, participants in the learning process. Comenius vacillates between portraying the teacher as a fountain of knowledge, a horse tamer, and a master technician. In his view, learners are containers into which knowledge is poured: They also can be blank sheets of paper, wild animals, loaves of bread, keys, or shoes. What are the roles of teachers and learners in contemporary language pedagogy?

CONFLICT OF SCIENCE AND RELIGION: AGAINST THE STUDIA HUMANITATIS

In Comenius's opinion, one of the major defects of the contemporary grammar schools is their total ignorance of the philosophy of observation inherent in the new science. Students spend their days translating obscure texts with the help of even more indecipherable commentaries. Comenius contends that students have no knowledge of the objects to which the Latin words refer. To remedy that situation, he advocates that students receive first-hand experience through their own senses of a particular object or event before they study it in the abstract: "It must be laid down as a general rule that each subject should be taught in combination with those which are correlative to it; that is to say, words should be studied in combination with the things to which they refer" (p. 177).

This overriding principle, that words and their meanings must remain intact, guides the entire curriculum, especially as it pertains to language instruction. Comenius continues: "Therefore, when instruction is given in any language, even in the mother-tongue itself, the words must be explained by reference to the objects that they denote" (p. 177). Words (i.e., language), Comenius contends, should never be used as mere vehicles by which to express grammatical concepts: modifier, ablative, first conjugation verb. Instruction in science—typically outside the purview of the language class— should not be alinguistic: "and contrariwise, the scholars must be taught to express in language whatever they see, hear, handle, or taste, so that their command of language, as it progresses, may ever run parallel to the growth of the understanding" (p. 177). To reiterate, "The scholar should be trained to express everything that he sees in words, and should be taught the meaning of all the words that he uses and this end can only be attained when *instruction in language goes hand in hand with instruction in facts"* (p. 177, emphasis mine).

The notion that language and subject matter are best taught and learned simultaneously mirrors the ideas expressed by Guarino and Ignatius. However, on the strength of Comenius's virulent criticism of contemporary education, it must be surmised that the *studia humanitatis* had failed to be instituted in the way in which they were initially intended: Namely, language teaching and instruction in history, moral philosophy, and geography should proceed in tandem. Moreover, Comenius's insistence on the introduction of science (i.e., the study of natural phenomena) into the curriculum must have been considered an innovation, even though we know from the writings of Vergerius that it was intended to be part of the *studia humanitatis* all along. In practice, however, humanities came to be understood only as rhetoric and dialectics, preceded by instruction in grammatical rules. In truth, what fundamentally distinguishes Comenius from the humanists is neither his belief that content and language should be taught together, nor the addition of "science" as an area of study, but rather his dismissal of the classical texts, and ancient authors as authorities.

Two chapters of *The Great Didactic* are devoted to Comenius's passionate denial of the usefulness of the classical authors. He attacks the humanist curriculum at its foundation, first by denying the wisdom of the past. He asks:

> Why do we allow ourselves to be led astray by the opinions of other men, when what is sought is a knowledge of the true nature of things? Have we nothing better to do than to follow others to their crossroads and down their byways? (...) Why should we use the eyes of other men in preference to our own? (p. 148).

The new science dictates that it is better to discover for oneself what is and isn't true than to rely on secondary sources:

> We arrive therefore at the following conclusion: Men must, as far as is possible, be taught to become wise by studying the heavens, the earth, oaks, and beeches, but not by studying books; that is to say, they must learn to know and investigate the things themselves, and not the observations that other people have made about the things (p. 150).

Because he believes that the certainty of knowledge can only be assured through direct experience of the evidence, he states "as a law" that "no information should be imparted on the grounds of bookish authority" (p. 150). In addition, Comenius advises that "the analytic method should never be used exclusively; in fact, preponderance should rather be given to the synthetic (discovery) method" (p. 150). Comenius denies that the past has a role in the present and, therefore, the applicability of history for the contemporary age. After all, the ancients had been proved wrong and thus had lost their magisterial function. Besides, why should students rely on someone else's opinions when they could discover the truth for themselves?

Comenius's aversion to the classical texts runs deeper than their apparent incongruence within a new scientific paradigm of observation and experimentation. He vehemently objects to the immoral and lascivious content of some of the authors. Such a reaction is expected from a deeply religious man; in fact, it is shared by humanists like Guarino and Ignatius. However, unlike the Christian humanists and even Luther himself who believed that worthwhile moral content could be found even in the study of non-Christian authors, Comenius cannot reconcile within his pedagogy the fact that the ancients were pagans. He is convinced that the objective of instilling moral values and piety in students is better served by the total abandonment of the ancient authors: "If we wish our schools to be truly Christian schools, the crowd of Pagan writers must be removed from them" (p. 231).

Comenius bases his argument on religious grounds. From the premise that children should be educated as "citizens of heaven," he derives the conclusion that they should study Christian, not pagan, figures (p. 232). In another barb in the direction of the Jesuits, he asserts:

> We see that the chief schools profess Christ in name only, but hold in highest esteem writers like Terence, Plautus, Cicero, Ovid, Catullus, and Tibullus. (...) For with the most learned men, even with theologians, the upholders of divine wisdom, the external mask only is supplied by Christ, while the spirit that pervades them is drawn from Aristotle and the host of heathen writers (p. 231).

Deriving his authority from other texts, Comenius provides citations from both the Bible and the early church fathers to support his position, claiming that "God expressly forbade His chosen people to have anything to do with the learning or the customs of the heathen," and quoting Cassiodorus to the effect that "the Scriptures are a heavenly school, a guide through life, the only true source of information" (p. 233).

His diatribe is so long and bitter that it is amazing that Comenius can recommend any ancient author at all. Nonetheless, he does mention a few who may still be included in the curriculum, but with a significant proviso:

> If any pagan writers are to be countenanced, let them be Seneca, Epictetus, Plato, and similar teachers of virtue and honesty; since in these comparatively little error and superstition are to be found, but even these books should not be given to the young until their Christian faith is well assured; and in any case careful editions should be issued in which the names of the gods and the general tone of superstition should be removed (p. 245).

Not unexpectedly, Comenius ends the chapter with a stunning reversal, stating that the ancient authors are not to be totally abandoned after all:

> Let there be no misunderstanding. We do not absolutely prohibit Christians from reading heathen writings, since to those who believe Christ has given the power of taking up serpents and drinking deadly things with impunity (p. 245).

Reading the classical authors is akin to handling poisonous snakes! They may be read, but they should be treated with utmost caution and preferably given only to older, more adept readers after they have developed a system of immunity.

Having rejected the classical texts as the basis for his curriculum, we can understand how new materials, in the form of the *Janua* and the *Vestibulum*, came to play such an important role in Comenius's vision for school reform. If language and content were to be taught hand in hand, but the content which formed the basis of the *studia humanitatis* was rejected, what then would replace it? This dilemma is one that Comenius could not resolve. In fact, notwithstanding his protestations, the study of ancient authors remains paramount in his proposed curriculum for the Latin School.

Ultimately what Comenius contends is that all normal children can learn languages; they need not be either geniuses or from privileged social milieux. The key to effective instruction is in combining language learning with instruction in interesting, relevant subject matter. In this respect, Comenius's basic theory corresponds precisely with that of Guarino and Ignatius. He disagrees over whether Latin and the *studia humanitatis* meet the requirements for suitable content, especially for children. What he fails to do is demonstrate the viability of his theory by providing examples of teaching practice which reflect that theory. He much more closely resembles Battista and the *Ratio* in his recommendations for language teaching practice, than he does Guarino or Ignatius in their pedagogical visions.

---

*P*ause to consider . . .

that there has always been considerable debate about the appropriateness of materials for children. Look at your state's guidelines for the publishing of foreign language materials for use in the elementary and secondary schools. To what extent does censorship exist? How do the guidelines affect the way the second language culture is transmitted to the students?

THE METHOD OF LANGUAGES

"Languages are learned," Comenius asserts, "not as forming in themselves a part of erudition or wisdom, but as being the means by which we may acquire knowledge and may impart it to others" (p. 203). Because language is fundamentally a means of communication rather than an academic discipline, it follows that there is no reason to learn any language in which one does not need to communicate. Languages—or for that matter any other subjects—are not studied for esoteric reasons, since "nothing is more useless than to learn and to know much, if such knowledge be of no avail for practical purposes" (p. 180). Therefore, Comenius argues that the choice of languages to include in the curriculum must be based on their practical utility for the learner:

> Not all languages should be learned, for this would be impossible; nor many, for this would be useless and would waste time that might be devoted to the acquisition of practical information; but only those that are necessary. Now necessary languages are these: the vernacular, for use at home, and the languages of the adjoining countries, for the sake of holding intercourse with neighbours. Thus for the Poles, German would be necessary; for others, the Hungarian, Wallachian, or Turkish languages. For the reading of serious books Latin is also advisable, as it is the common language of the learned. For philosophers and physicians, Greek and Arabic; and for theologians, Greek and Hebrew (p. 203).

Thus, Comenius's case for the study of foreign languages by the masses parallels our modern understanding that language is first a system of communication. The study of Latin, conversely, has become the exclusive prerogative of a fossilized intellectual elite.

Comenius also recognizes that the skills that students need to develop depend upon their intended use of the language, whether to speak with native speakers or to read texts, and that instruction should focus on the development of necessary skills only:

> Not all these languages should be learned thoroughly, but only so far as is necessary. It is not necessary to speak (biblical) Greek or Hebrew as fluently as the mother tongue, since there are no people with whom we can converse in those languages. It suffices to learn them well enough to be able to read and understand books written in them (p. 203).

This point, too, is congruent with one of the basic principles underlying Comenius's methodology: Namely, "the task of schools will be rendered easier if the subjects taught be curtailed. This can be done if omission be made

(i) of all unnecessary matter; (ii) of all unsuitable matter; (iii) of all minute detail" (p. 180). With regard to language learning, he insists:

> The complete and detailed knowledge of a language, no matter which it be, is quite unnecessary, and it is absurd and useless on the part of anyone to try to attain it. Not even Cicero (who is considered the greatest master of the Latin language) was acquainted with all its details, since he confessed that he was ignorant of the words used by artisans (p. 204).

The manner by which to acquire requisite functional proficiency in a language, whether expressive or interpretive, does not occur from the study of rules or mindless repetition:

> The study of languages, especially in youth, should be joined to that of objects, that our acquaintance with the objective world and with language, that is to say, our knowledge of facts and our power to express them, may progress side by side. For it is men that we are forming and not parrots (p. 203-4).

Rather than through precepts or drills, language and content (i.e., form and meaning together) must provide the focus of instruction: "From this it follows, firstly, that words should not be learned apart from the objects to which they refer" (p. 204-5). With the added specification that the subject matter must be both appealing to the students and age appropriate, Comenius explains that this basic notion of the interdependence of language and content instruction motivated him in his textbook writing: "It was this consideration that led me to publish the *Janua Linguarum*; in which words, arranged in sentences, explain the nature of objects, and, as it is said, with no small success" (p. 204).

AN ECLECTIC METHOD, A MULTIPLICITY OF CONTRADICTIONS

Comenius conveniently provides a list of eight rules which "will render the acquisition of the various languages an easy matter" (p. 205). Based on the requirement that only useful languages should be studied, the rules detail specific languages. His obsession with efficiency entailed that one of the rules circumscribe the "definite space of time allotted" to each language (p. 205). It is not surprising to discover the mandate that the mother tongue must be learned first. Although it may seem blatantly obvious to the modern reader, this recommendation was necessary to ensure first language literacy skills. Once having mastered the native language, "since it is intimately connected with the gradual unfolding of the objective world to the senses, necessarily requires several years (I should say eight to ten, or the whole of childhood with a part of boyhood," the child should then learn the language of the neighboring country, "and then the language that may have to be used in its (the mother tongue's) place, I mean that of the neighboring nation (for I am of opinion that modern languages should be commenced before the learned ones) (...) each of which can be sufficiently mastered in one year" (p. 205). Only after these two languages are acquired should the study of Latin begin: "Then Latin may be learned, and after Latin, Greek, Hebrew, etc." (p. 205). How long should all of this take? Comenius calculates that "Latin can be learned in two years, Greek in one year, and Hebrew in six months" (p. 205-6).

Under his school organization plan, languages are studied in order of practical import: the mother tongue is studied in the Vernacular School, followed by the modern languages, while the Latin School provides instruction in the three classical languages. Comenius advises languages be studied one at a time to avoid confusion (p. 205). The clearly delineated sequence and rigid timetable for instruction are in full accord with his desire to present a system of education that runs like a well-designed machine. However, in the specific descriptions of what instruction within this system looks like, contradictions soon multiply.

The third rule for effective language teaching is that "all languages are easier to learn by practice than from rules" (p. 206). Throughout the treatise, Comenius argues that children learn from experience rather than from norms. From this, he concludes: "In schools, therefore, let the students learn to write by writing, to talk by talking, to sing by singing, and to reason by reasoning" (p. 195). Rules, conversely, are seldom helpful. In fact, he states the following:

> Rules are like thorns to the understanding, and to grasp their meaning needs both attention and ability, while even the dullest students are aided by example. *No one has ever mastered any language or art by precept alone; while by practice this is possible, even without precept* (p. 196, emphasis mine).

Only a particular kind of student can benefit from precepts, and even they acquire language easily without them. Having convincingly just made this point, Comenius's next three rules are surprising: They all promote the study of rules:

> (iv) But rules assist and strengthen the knowledge derived from practice. (v) The rules to which language are reduced should be grammatical and not philosophic. (vi) In writing rules for the new language, the one already known must be continually kept in mind, so that stress may be laid only on the points in which the languages differ (p. 206).

With regard to the fifth directive, Comenius explains that rules "should simply state what is correct and how the constructions should be made" and leave out "the causes and antecedents of words, phrases, and sentences;" that is, they should be strictly regulatory and not explain why a construction is necessary (p. 206). This complements the earlier advice that rules should be "short," "as simple as possible," and "of perpetual use" (p. 200); however, it is in direct opposition to the recommendation that students "should learn, and learn thoroughly, the etymology of all words, the reasons for all constructions, and the principles on which the rules for the various subjects of study have been formed" (p. 154). Comenius provides two examples of the kind of explanation that teachers should supply:

> For instance, if the question arose whether it would be more correct to say *totus populus* or *cunctus populus*, and the teacher were merely to say "*cunctus populus* is the right phrase," but omitted to give any reason, the pupil would soon forget it. If, on the other hand, he were to say "*Cunctus* is a contraction for *conjunctus*, and therefore *totus* should be used when the object denoted is homogeneous, *cunctus* when the conception is collective, as here," it is scarcely conceivable that the pupil could forget it, unless his intelligence were very limited. Again, if the grammatical question were to arise why we say *mea refert, tua refert*, but *ejus refert*; that is to say, why we use the ablative (as it is supposed to be) in the first and second persons, but the genitive in the third person; if I were to answer, that *refert* is a contraction for *res fert*, and that the phrases are therefore *mea res fert, tua res fert, ejus res fert* (or in their contracted form *mea refert, tua refert, ejus refert*), and that therefore *mea* and *tua* are not the ablative but the nominative, would not the pupil be stimulated to further efforts? (p. 153).

How reminiscent this passage is of Battista and of the casuistry of the *Ratio*!

The sixth rule appears to foreshadow contrastive analysis. Rather than learn from direct experience with the second language, Comenius now maintains that it is a mistake "if boys are given a foreign teacher who does not understand their language" (p. 134). He advocates using an approach that is specific to the students' native languages, claiming that students must have access to bilingual dictionaries with entries in their first language, followed by Latin equivalents—and not vice versa—because students want "to learn Latin through the medium of the language they already know" (p. 134).

With the seventh rule, suddenly Comenius abandons both the humanists and his own countless statements that the acquisition of language and content area knowledge proceed simultaneously:

> (vii.) The first exercises in a new language must deal with subject matter that is already familiar. Otherwise the mind will have to pay attention to words and to things at the same time, and will thus be distracted and weakened. Its efforts should therefore be confined to words, that it may master them easily and quickly (p. 207).

No explanation exists for this amazing about-face. The incongruence between his earlier statements of theory and his recommendations for practice, however, does not stop here.

Comenius concludes with the eighth rule in which he again expresses his commitment to method: "(viii) All languages, therefore, can be learned by method. That is to say, by practice, combined with rules of a very simple nature that only refer to points of difference with the language already known, and by exercises that refer to some familiar subject" (p. 207). If Comenius's prose appears to be confused it is because his method is not coherent. A theory of language teaching that views language learning as a result of meaning-driven communicative experience based on interaction with interesting content is combined with classroom practice that consists of memorization, form-focused drills, and repetition, with a fastidious emphasis on accuracy.

The advent of the printing press greatly diminished the necessity of memorizing passages in order to have them at hand. Yet the practice of memorization must have been so deeply ingrained in classroom practice that it could not go unmentioned in Comenius's method. He criticizes contemporary teachers who "fall into error" by giving boys "endless dictations" and who "make them learn their lessons off by heart" (p. 120). He warns the reader that memorization must not be carried to an extreme, resulting in students who "are overburdened with dictations, with exercises, and with lessons that they have to commit to memory, until nausea and, in some cases, insanity is produced" (pp. 136-37). However, once again, in the chapter immediately following the one in which the latter quote appears, Comenius backtracks from this position on memorization and calls for abundant memorization as the foundation of academic success. He states axiomatically its central importance in education: "For that only which has been thoroughly understood, and committed to memory as well, can be called the property of the mind" (p. 152). In one set of instructions for the use of the *Vestibulum* and the *Janua*, he specifies that they too should be memorized!

Comenius's comments with regard to repetition and drill were often cited by the language teaching historians of the 1960s. Such recommendations tied in perfectly with the audiolingual approach in which exact imitation of the model was advocated: "At first the prescribed form should be imitated with exactness" (p. 198). This maxim is followed in fact by a perfect description of pattern substitution drills:

(This is the model) if any construction or sentence extracted from a classic writer have to be imitated. If the original phrase be "Rich in possessions," the boy should be made to imitate it by saying, "Rich in coins," "Rich in moneys," "Rich in flocks" "Rich in vineyards. "When Cicero says, "In the opinion of the most learned men, Eudemus easily holds the first place in astrology," this may be copied with very little alteration as "In the opinion of the greatest orators, Cicero easily holds the first place in eloquence," "In the opinion of the whole Church, St. Paul easily holds the first place in Apostleship." (p. 199).

Not only oral pattern drills are advocated as useful, but also repeated copying of text as well: "It will be of great advantage to read and copy the declensions and conjugations over and over again, until, by this means reading, writing, the meaning of words, and the formation of the case endings, have been thoroughly learned" (p. 178).

Just as the Jesuits had done in the *Ratio*, Comenius recommends the act of teaching someone else as an excellent way to improve one's own understanding of a topic. However, the example he provides to illustrate how this may be accomplished leaves the reader doubtful that he has ever tried this with students. It also runs contrary to his earlier position on mindless repetition (that we are training men, not parrots):

> It might be done in the following way: In each lesson, after the teacher has briefly gone through the work that has been prepared, and has explained the meanings of the words, one of the pupils should be allowed to rise from his place and repeat what has just been said in the same order (just as if he were the teacher of the rest), to give his explanations in the same words, and to employ the same examples, and if he make a mistake he should be corrected. Then another can be called up and made go through the same performance while the rest listen. After him a third, a fourth, and as many as are necessary, until it is evident that all have understood the lesson and are in a position to explain it. In carrying this out great care should be taken to call up the clever boys first, in order that, after their example, the stupid ones may find it easier to follow (p. 157).

Comenius actually believes that students will find this exercise riveting, "since the scholars may, at any time, be called up and asked to repeat what the teacher has said, each of them will be afraid of breaking down and appearing ridiculous before the others, and will therefore attend carefully and allow nothing to escape him" (pp. 157-58). Disregarding the fact that the teacher resorts to shame and ridicule to motivate students, as the argument progresses, Comenius appears to lose sight of the fact that the point of his argument was the benefit of teaching others and begins instead to relate the benefits of repetition: "By means of such constant repetition the scholars will gain a better acquaintance with the subject than they could possibly obtain by private study" (p. 158). In this section, we also find a variation on the Jesuits' suggestion that students meet in small groups to discuss the day's lesson. In Comenius's version, however, one of the students should "take the place of teacher and control the proceedings" (p. 158).

Whereas earlier in the treatise Comenius had advocated that "the study of a new language be allowed to proceed gradually and in such a way that the scholar learn first to understand (for this is the easiest), then to write (for here there is time for consideration), and lastly to speak (which is the hardest, because the process is so rapid)" (pp. 134-35), he now emphasizes the importance of accuracy from the beginning:

> The first attempt at imitation should be as accurate as possible, that not the smallest deviation from the model be made. (...) For whatever comes first is, as it were, the foundation of that which follows. If the foundation be firm, a solid edifice can be constructed upon it, but if it be weak this is impossible. Those, therefore, who are learning any art should take care to make themselves masters of the rudiments by imitating their copies accurately (pp. 199-200).

This entire passage, down to the use of absolute terms, is reminiscent of Battista. Of course, the insistence on accuracy implies that a discussion of correction must follow. The reader is not disappointed.

---

*P*ause to consider . . .

that an emphasis on accuracy from the beginning is based on the notion that learners will be forever unable to "correct" errors once they are committed, much like a vicious habit is extremely difficult—if not impossible—to break. This approach is in direct opposition to one in which errors are viewed as a natural part of a learner's developing competence, with their gradual diminishment as the learner progresses. The way errors are treated, then, can suggest either moral rectitude or lassitude on the part of the teacher. What does either position imply about the learner?

THE TEACHER, IN PRACTICE

Comenius presents widely vacillating pictures of the teacher: from the mother bird to the horse tamer. He repeats these same images in reference to correction and discipline. Teachers should be "gentle and persuasive" (p. 130). Their instructions should include clear explanations "relieved by a humorous or at any rate by a less serious tone" (p. 131). Before they expect students to perform, however, teachers should explain the point thoroughly, give clear directions for the task, provide helpful hints in the beginning, and be patient. "No blows should be given for a lack of readiness to learn" (p. 139). Again, Comenius stresses that it is the teacher's fault when students cannot complete an assigned task; they merely haven't been sufficiently prepared.

One way by which to prepare students to receive new information is through the teacher's careful presentation of the new material in an "entertaining" manner such that the pupils' interest is stimulated (p. 167). This may be accomplished, Comenius contends, by making clear the link between what learners have previously studied and the new subject: for example, socratically, by asking questions. "For, if the scholar's ignorance of the subject be mercilessly exposed, he may be fired with a desire to master it and understand it thoroughly" (p. 167). To maintain the students' attention during the presentation of new material, the teacher, while standing on an elevated platform where all can see him, should demand repetition of what he says:

> (The teacher should say) "Tell me (mentioning some boy), what have I just said? Repeat that sentence! Tell me; how have I reached this point?" (...) If any pupil be found who is not paying attention, he should be reprimanded or punished on the spot. In this way the scholars will be made keen and attentive (p. 167).

When the student questioned cannot answer, the teacher asks another student, and then another, and another "without repeating the question" until he finds one who has paid attention and can answer (p. 167). He praises those who answer well and corrects those who make mistakes. When the lesson is over, the students ask questions, but only in front of the whole class so that everyone can benefit from the answers (p. 168). Students should also correct each other's work, which saves the teacher's time; in a way, this is identical to the "concertatio" proposed by the Jesuits in which one students reads his translation while a rival listens for errors (pp. 169-70).

All of this does not imply that students who fail to respond correctly are treated gently. "There is a proverb in Bohemia," Comenius writes:

> "A school without discipline is like a mill without water," and this is very true. For, if you withdraw the water from a mill, it stops, and, in the same way, if you deprive a school of discipline, you take away from it its motive power. (...) It must not be thought, however, that we wish our schools to resound with shrieks and with blows. What we demand is vigilance and attention on the part of the master and of the pupils (p. 249).

It has already been suggested that students remain attentive either through the teacher's gentle persuasion and humor or by embarrassment. Comenius differentiates between errors in morality, for which the discipline must be "severe," and those in grammar. He suggests the following disciplines for students who err in their schoolwork:

> Sometimes a few severe words or a reprimand before the whole class is very efficacious, while sometimes a little praise bestowed on the others has great effect. "See how well so-and-so attends! See how quickly he sees the point! While you sit there like a stone!" It is often of use to laugh at the backward ones. "You silly fellow, can't you understand such a simple matter?" (pp. 250-51).

These then are "kinds of punishment suitable for boys who are free-born and of normal disposition, and these we may employ" (p. 254). However, he concedes that for some, beating is the only discipline that renders the desired effect (p. 252).

The reason for punishment is clearly stated: "It is not because they have erred that they should be punished (for what has been done cannot be undone), but in order that they may not err again in the future" (p. 249). For this reason, "errors must be corrected by the master on the spot; but precepts, that is to say the rules, and the exceptions to the rules, must be given at the same time" (p. 200).

Comenius's curriculum progresses according to a rigidly defined timetable prescribed for all students. He defines the solution to the schools' problems partly in terms of clear objectives: "goals to be reached by the scholars at the end of each year, month, or day" (p. 161). Furthermore, he argues that:

> The same method of instruction must be used for all the sciences, the same for all the arts, and the same for all languages. In each school the same arrangement and treatment should be adopted for all studies. The class books for each subject should, as far as possible, be of the same edition. In this way difficulties will be avoided and progress will be made easy (p. 141).

Obviously such a plan cannot accommodate a language learning theory that views language as communication (complex and messy), errors as developmental, or learners as individuals whose language skills develop at varying rates.

At some level, Comenius must have recognized the inconsistencies between his communicatively-based theory and his rule-based practice. Despite everything he had written previously, at the conclusion of his description of the Vernacular School, he offers the following advice:

> If any boys are to learn foreign languages, they should learn them now, at about the age of ten, eleven or twelve, that is to say, *between* the Vernacular School and the Latin School. The best way is to send them to the place where the language that they wish to learn is spoken, and in the new language to make them read, write, and learn the class books of the Vernacular School (p. 273).

In other words, the most effective way to acquire functional language proficiency is through contact with excellent linguistic models and meaningful interaction with interesting, relevant subject matter in the second language.

If this then were Comenius's ultimate advice to those who wish to learn a second language, why wouldn't it also be his recommendation for learning Latin as it was for Guarino and Ignatius? Comenius's response is clear and direct: The reason is that "my method has not as its sole object the Latin language, that nymph on whom such unbounded admiration is generally wasted, but seeks a way by which each modern language may be taught as well" (p. 267). As far as he is concerned Latin is no longer a functional language. To those who may argue that students in the Vernacular School should at least learn technical terms in Latin, because they will just have to learn them later anyway in the Latin School, Comenius replies:

> Let the *learned* retain their own terms. We are now seeking a way by which *the common people* may be led to understand and take an interest in the liberal arts and sciences; and with this end in view we must not speak in a language that is *foreign* to them, and that is in itself *artificial*" (p. 271, emphasis mine).

The humanists, therefore, were not wrong in attempting to teach Latin to children before they were ready to learn a second language. Comenius agreed that 10-year-olds learn second languages without difficulty. They were not mistaken in proposing the second language, Latin, as the medium of instruction. According to Comenius, the reason that Latin could not be taught like any modern language is that the goal of that instruction had changed: No need existed to develop functional proficiency in a language that no longer functioned.

---

*P*ause to consider . . .
_____

that consistent with pansophic philosophy, Comenius insists on universalism; that everyone acquire the same knowledge in the same way using the same materials. To what extent do second or foreign language programs share the same goals? Who sets those goals? How are the objectives of individual learners met? What about teachers?

The final irony of Comenius's *Great Didactic* lay in his description of the curriculum for the Latin School: "In this school the pupils should learn four languages (one modern, Latin, Greek, and Hebrew) and acquire an encyclopedic knowledge of the (seven liberal) arts" (p. 274). Students receive training in grammar, dialectics, rhetoric, arithmetic, geometry, music, and astronomy. To these, he adds physics, geography, chronology, history, morality, and theology. The curriculum is divided into six classes, in order from lowest to highest: grammar, natural philosophy, mathematics, ethics, dialects, and rhetoric. Comenius's curriculum reflects precisely the format of the dreaded Jesuit school! One final contradiction, however, is in store. With his diatribe against the classical authors apparently forgotten, Comenius ends the chapter with the following recommendation:

> We will only touch on one point further. An acquaintance with history is the most important element in a man's education, and is, as it were, the eye of his whole life. This subject, therefore, should be taught in each of the six classes that our pupils may be ignorant of no event which has happened from ancient times to the present day; but its study must be arranged in such a way that it lighten their work instead of increasing it, and serve as a relaxation after their severer labours (p. 280).

Thus, Latin and history, the first subjects of the *studia humanitatis*, form the core curriculum of Comenius's Latin School.

CONCLUSION

In many ways, Comenius was a man sandwiched between competing paradigms: the scientific and the religious. He appreciated the discoveries of the new science and yet he could not abandon Aristotle. When he tried to adopt the new scientific model in his pedagogical argumentation, he substituted medieval analogies for true observation and experimentation. From a religious perspective, too, he could not reconcile the inclusion of the ancient pagan authors within a strict orthodox framework. Yet he couldn't justify their total abandonment either. He argued against the Jesuit system and adopted many of its features.

As much as he struggled to create a single, uniform method for language teaching, Comenius was torn between a theory that considered language a system of communication—a way of exchanging meaning—and a teaching practice that relied on inflexible lesson plans, absolute accuracy, and lockstep progress. To the modern reader, he may seem either schizophrenic or eager to please everyone. Maybe this is why he is one of most cited historical figures in language teaching—for in his writing one can find support for any pedagogical stance. The most hardlined methodologist offers the most eclectic method of all.

As we have seen, Comenius, Ignatius, and Guarino shared many beliefs about language learning. Together they represent a consistent, traditional theory of language teaching. Although Guarino's and Ignatius's beliefs about language learning were misconstrued by son and committee, respectively, Comenius's theory was corrupted within himself as he attempted to transmit it into pedagogical directives. Because he fails to identify teaching practices that are congruent with his theoretical stance, the methodology he proposes ultimately results in incoherence. Just as Ignatius's theory fails to be expressed in the *Ratio* and Guarino's vision cannot be found in Battista's treatise, similarly from Comenius's methodology alone, no way exists to reconstruct his underlying theory.

---

*P*ause to consider . . .

that despite the convenience of well-designed and readily available materials, some teachers still balk at being told to do "x, y, and z" without any explanation as to why such materials are better than what they've used in the past. Examine the language textbook you currently use. How easy is it to identify the underlying theory of second language acquisition on which it is based? How well do the exercises and activities reflect the principles of that theory?

CHAPTER FOUR

The Applied Linguist: Theory and Teaching Practice

Theory, says Vives, is easy and short, but has no result other than the gratification that it affords. Practice, on the other hand, is difficult and prolix, but is of immense utility.

—Quoted by Comenius in *The Great Didactic*, 1657

There is nothing so practical as good theory.

—Kurt Lewin, social psychologist, 1951 quoted by H. H. Stern, *Fundamental Concepts of Language Teaching*, 1983

It was only during the latter portion of Comenius's lifetime, in 1649, that English officially replaced Latin as the language for all legal documents in Great Britain. Less than 250 years later, Comenius's biographer commented on the powerful position that Latin once held as the language of international communication by stating "the student who could talk and write in the tongue of Cicero possessed a means of communication with kindred spirits throughout the world, *unequalled in universality by any language of the present day*" (Keatinge 1896, pp. 17-18, emphasis mine). At the beginning of the twentieth century, the thought that another language could ever gain the influence and status that Latin once boasted was inconceivable. Yet, in the course of the past 100 years, and less than 300 years after it was proclaimed the official government language in Great Britain, English has become the language of wider communication throughout the world.

Because English is now *de facto* the international language for commerce, scholarship, and technology, the language teaching profession today finds itself in much the same situation as did Guarino and the early humanists with Latin in the fifteenth century, magnified to encompass a much larger population on an even grander geographical scale. Millions of people from every corner of the planet seek to acquire fluency in this second, world language. Interest in acquiring competence in languages other than English is also flourishing, especially with the multilingual situation in Europe, Spanish in the United States, and French in Canada. Contemporary examples of recurrent difficulties in transmitting theory in practice, however, suggest that the problem of implementation is far from resolved.

P<small>ause to consider</small> . . .

given the similarities in the functional contexts, whether a parallel exists between the pedagogy proposed by the educators who sought to reform the teaching of Latin with the aim to develop interpretive and expressive second language skills in fifteenth- and sixteenth-century learners and the language teaching practices advocated by twentieth-century reformers. In what ways does current second language teaching theory purport many of the same beliefs held by the historical reformers, now that the prevalent goal of instruction is once again the development of functional language ability?

THE PAST AS A TOOL FOR THE PRESENT

A little more than thirty years ago, interest in the history of language teaching briefly surged in the United States. Within the span of a decade, several volumes appeared that professed a historical perspective (Mackey 1965; Titone 1968; Kelly 1969). The scholarly enthusiasm in diachronic research was not coincidental, rather it arose in response to a highly touted language teaching methodology known as "audiolingualism," or the "New Key." Proponents of the method scrambled to cite historical evidence in favor of the new "scientific" pedagogy. To that purpose, any references to "habit formation," "reinforcement," "repetition," "automaticity," "mimicry," and "memorization" were culled from old pedagogical treatises. Battista, the *Ratio* of the Jesuits, and Comenius were among the popular sources. Despite the attempt to bolster its validity by tracing its "traditional" origins, the method itself—although initially embraced with much enthusiasm by the language teaching profession—quickly met its demise as it failed to produce the fluent second language users it had promised.

At about the same time, a counter-movement was forming against a behaviorist approach to language acquisition. In 1978, a different sort of history of foreign language teaching emerged in a small volume entitled *The Language Teaching Controversy* (Diller, 1978). Based on Chomsky's (1965) distinction between "empiricist" and "rationalist" positions on language acquisition, Diller provides a parallel framework for distinguishing two distinct approaches to language teaching. The empiricist position is defined as one that views language learning as "a kind of habit formation through conditioning and drill" (Diller, p. 6). Within this theoretical framework, language teaching practice is commonly referred to as "mim-mem," mimicry and memorization. In its extreme interpretation, language acquisition within this perspective is nothing more than a trained stimulus-response in the purest behaviorist sense. This is the theory on which audiolingualism was based. Conversely, the rationalist position is described as follows:

> In the rationalist camp there has been more variety in teaching methods, ranging from the ill-conceived grammar-translation methods, through Gouin's highly original "series method" to the tightly organized "direct methods" of Berlitz and de Sauzé. From the very first day, the direct methods have the students generate original and meaningful sentences in order for them to gain a functional knowledge of the rules of grammar (Diller, pp. 6-7).

Diller details the theoretical consistency between the second, rationalist, position and Chomsky's theory of transformational generative grammar.

Because the point here is to investigate what is meant by "traditional" language teaching and how it relates to theory, it is important to note Diller's claim regarding the relationship between empiricism and rationalism in the history of language teaching:

> It should seem obvious that the history of foreign language teaching did not have a linear development. We do not have a situation in which the faults of one method were corrected by a new method,

each one superseding the last. Rather, we have two separate histories. The great theoretical division between linguists—the empiricists vs. the rationalists—also divides the language teaching methodologies (Diller, p. 5).

The historical evidence prior to 1880 certainly supports the notion that language teaching pedagogy has not evolved in an amelioratory fashion, with each generation improving on the methods of its predecessor. The comparison of the pedagogical manuals of Battista and the *Ratio* with the beliefs held by Guarino and Ignatius, in addition to the inconsistencies in Comenius's work, suggest that subsequent generations would have been unable to reconstruct the theory of second language acquisition held by the reformers. Nonetheless, Diller concludes:

> Viewed, then, from the standpoint of theory, the history of foreign language teaching begins to take intelligible shape. We have two major traditions of language teaching, based on two different views of language and language acquisition. Decisions on language teaching methodology have not been primarily the result of practical and disinterested experimentation; they have been decisions based instead on differing theories of language (Diller, p. 8).

To some extent, I agree with Diller's assessment of an ongoing dichotomy in the history of language teaching; namely, two traditions exist. Where our conclusions diverge is in the characterization of the relationship between the two traditions. Diller believes that the dual traditions are a result of two opposing theoretical perspectives, each advancing independently of the other:

> Two very different theories of how languages are learned, then, have fostered two very different conceptions of how foreign languages ought to be taught. The history of language teaching methodology, like the history of linguistic theory, is a dual history—each stream having its own separate development (Diller, p. 8).

Rather than two opposing theories existing in tandem, Battista, the *Ratio*, and Comenius each insisted that their pedagogical recommendations were accurate representations of a single theory. Thus, the historical evidence—except during the brief hiatus of audiolingualism—suggests that the problem lies, not in differing theories per se, but in how one consistent theory has repeatedly failed to be conveyed to practitioners.

A curious and perplexing aspect of Diller's argument is his placement of "grammar-translation methods" into the rationalist camp, as it is instead the empiricist position that emphasizes those aspects of instruction usually associated with "traditional" language teaching: a reliance on the students' first language as the medium of instruction, repeated practice of structural patterns, memorization of grammatical rules, first language-second language translation, and an early and ongoing insistence on structural accuracy. One explanation for this classification may well be strategic: the use of "history" to support a theoretical position. What is missing from Diller's thesis is any historical evidence to support his contention or refute that of the behaviorists. His blanket characterization of language teaching prior to 1880 as "ill-conceived grammar-translation methods" seriously undermines his argument.

History and tradition are powerful forces in academic discourse, and Diller is no different from the proponents of the New Key, or even the early humanists, when he enlists that authority. It is a timeworn practice in the profession. To develop a case for content-based second language instruction, Brinton, Snow and Wesche (1989) quote St. Augustine (as cited in Kelly) to lend credence to their argument. Likewise, Savignon (1983) enlists the text of Montaigne and quotes selected passages of Comenius to persuade the reader to favor communicative language teaching. In one of the most popular pedagogical manuals of the day, *Teaching Language in Context*, Omaggio (1986) asserts:

> This book is not designed to raise new dust. It does not propose yet another revolutionary theory of language acquisition or promote new methodologies. Rather, it seeks to extract from our rich heritage of resources and practices those elements that seem most sound and to suggest a way to organize that knowledge and expertise so we can maximize opportunities for the development of proficiency among our students (Omaggio, pp. xi-xii).

In much the same way as Battista disavows his own hand in the content of his treatise—insisting that it is his father's expertise and experience that he is merely reproducing—modern applied linguists claim that their directives are not merely their own or even twentieth-century inventions, rather that they derive from "tradition," "history," and "our rich heritage of resources and practices." Before the profession can rightly usurp tradition, however, the historical evidence provokes the reassessment of what exactly constitutes "tradition" in language teaching.

Pause to consider . . .

that, until now, "traditional" language teaching has remained either undefined or used to refer only to those practices advocated by Battista and the *Ratio*, not to Guarino and Ignatius. Conversely, Comenius has been quoted to support any position on pedagogy. How has the historical evidence presented here altered our understanding of "traditional" language teaching?

FIRST, A REDEFINITION OF "TRADITIONAL" LANGUAGE TEACHING

The second language teaching theory shared by Guarino Guarini, Ignatius of Loyola, and Johannes Comenius views language as, above all, a system of communication. This principal characteristic informs their objectives for instruction, as well as its means. When Latin was still the language of wider communication among the educated peoples of Europe, a curriculum that would create fluent users of Latin was at once immensely practical and highly desirable. Thus, second language instruction had as its ultimate goal the development of functional language ability in the learners. Such ability included—for Guarino and Ignatius—expressive skills, both oral and written, in addition to interpretive competence. For Comenius, in whose time oral fluency in Latin had become obsolete, the development of specific interpretive skills alone was deemed sufficient as the majority of students needed only the ability to read Latin texts. Regardless of the changing status of Latin within the larger society, all three reformers concurred on certain fundamental characteristics of the second language program, which ensured that learners in the classroom setting would acquire functional second language competence.

First, all interaction, both instructional and recreational, in class and out, between students and teachers, and among students themselves, was conducted entirely in the second language. Interestingly, this condition was mandated even though Latin was the native language of neither the teachers nor the students. The exclusive use of the second language was considered so essential to the acquisition process that it was advocated even in the beginning classes with the sole stipulation that teachers accommodate their speech to make its meaning accessible to early-stage language learners. Language learners gained functional communicative ability by using the second language to communicate in multiple contexts and with varied interlocutors.

Second, the entire curriculum was based on learners' interpretation of interesting texts. The oral texts consisted of the instructors' own second language discourse: in the form of lectures, accounts, explanations, and storytelling. The written texts were the classical authors themselves, edited perhaps for length and age-appropriate content, but otherwise unadulterated in their authenticity. The texts were selected for the interesting and edifying messages they conveyed. Because they were authentic texts (i.e., texts originally written for native readers and offered in their unabridged form), the language they presented to learners was filled with the richness, natural redundancy, and fluency of expression inherent to such discourse. Thus, in their pedagogical recommendations, the educators reaffirmed that the most effective way to develop communicative ability in a second language was to have students employ that language to understand and convey messages, oral and written. Because the content of such messages was the *studia humanitatis,* students in this instructional setting acquired language and subject-matter knowledge simultaneously.

On the one hand, the pedagogical directives that Guarino, Ignatius, and (at least in part) Comenius proposed are elegant in their simplicity: exclusive use of the second language, extensive use of authentic texts, and language study that proceeds hand-in-hand with instruction in content. On the other hand, as experienced language professionals themselves, they were also acutely aware of the complexity that the changes they proposed presented to the contemporary status quo. They realized that their approach would not banish entirely those peculiar features of second language discourse that teachers find particularly distressing: Namely, the learners' language, especially in the early stages, is rarely nativelike or error-free; although grammatical rules could be taught explicitly, their assimilation and integration into learners' developing linguistic systems seldom follows a smooth and direct path.

Therefore, given the disparity between what they understood the purpose of language instruction to be and the concerns that fellow teachers may have, the reformers were careful to explain those aspects of learners' second language development. They described second language acquisition as a gradual, developmental process through which individual learners move at varying rates. Because of this, teachers should not expect that all students will progress according to some pre-established, institutionally-set timetable. In addition, they reminded teachers and learners alike that nativelike levels of competence are attained only after years of engagement with the second language through the interpretation and expression of texts. It follows logically that the language of beginners will not resemble that of native speakers, and it should not be held to such standards. Nonetheless, the reformers fully expected students to eventually attain subject matter and language competence by using the second language as the medium, rather than the focus, of instruction.

All three reformers recognized that although learners' language inevitably contains mistakes as a result of the developmental nature of the acquisition process, language competence steadily improves with time, exposure to good models, and motivating circumstances. They argued that the refinement of second language skills is never-ending, citing their own second language experiences as evidence. Furthermore, they conceded that not all learners reach extraordinary levels of interpretive and expressive fluency, not because the acquisition of a second language is necessarily restricted to an elite talented few, but rather because many students either do not wish or cannot afford to invest the time and energy that such attainment demands.

Despite these beliefs about second language teaching and learning—a theory that remained remarkably consistent throughout at least three centuries of Western education—the methodologists who penned the pedagogical manuals in which such beliefs should have been transmitted to language professionals failed dismally in their task. In place of the reformers' stance, the reader of such documents finds instead very different advice:

A reliance on the learners' first language to convey messages;

An insistence on first language-second language translation throughout the program of language study;

A curriculum centered on explicit instruction in and memorization of grammatical rules with all their exceptions;

A focus on linguistic accuracy from the beginning;

The postponement of subject-matter teaching in the second language to the advanced classes; and,

An overall de-emphasis on the use of second language discourse, oral and written, especially in the early stages of acquisition.

In a textbook that is widely-used in second language teacher education programs, Brown (1993) summarizes language teaching prior to the eighteenth century as follows:

Latin was taught by means of what has been called the Classical Method: focus on grammatical rules, memorization of vocabulary and of various declensions and conjugations, translation of texts, doing written exercises (p. 16).

The author also claims that this method persisted for the teaching of foreign languages throughout the eighteenth and nineteenth centuries because

[l]ittle thought was given at the time to teaching oral use of languages; after all, languages were not taught primarily to learn oral/aural communication but to learn for the sake of being "scholarly" or, in some instances, for gaining a reading proficiency in a foreign language (p. 16).

Finally, he cites the major characteristics of the "Classical/Grammar Translation Method" as it remains today:

1. Classes are taught in the mother tongue, with little active use of the target language.
2. Much vocabulary is taught in the form of lists of isolated words.
3. Long elaborate explanations of the intricacies of grammar are given.
4. Grammar provides the rules for putting words together, and instruction often focuses on the form and inflection of words.
5. Reading of difficult classical texts is begun early.
6. Little attention is paid to the content of texts, which are treated as exercises in grammatical analysis.
7. Often the only drills are exercises in translating disconnected sentences from the target language into the mother tongue.
8. Little or no attention is given to pronunciation.
(Prator & Celce-Murcia 1979, p. 3; cited in Brown 1993, p. 16)

In as much as descriptions of "traditional language teaching" refer to the practices espoused in Battista's treatise or in the *Ratio* of the Jesuits, the depictions are correct. However, such characterizations do not reflect the *other* tradition in language teaching, that of the great educators who proposed the reform of classroom practices that failed to produce competent, fluent, proficient *users* of the second language. In neglecting to acknowledge the second, *innovative* tradition, the profession dismisses the best that Western education has had to offer. How is it possible that such a discrepancy between theory (and its implications for innovation in the curriculum) and practice persisted throughout three centuries of reform? Does it, in fact, remain a problem today?

---

*P*ause to consider . . .

what students would study if a language program were to remove the emphasis on formal aspects of grammar in the early courses. Would it necessarily "dummy down" the curriculum? As part of *their* reform, Guarino, Ignatius, and Comenius injected substantial "content" (i.e., history, geography, poetry, music, arithmetic, science) to provide a necessary intellectual challenge in the early stages of the curriculum. How would a similar change affect disciplinary boundaries in today's university?

"COMMUNICATIVE LANGUAGE TEACHING" THEORY AND CURRENT PEDAGOGY

The second language teaching theory advocated by educational reformers of the fifteenth, sixteenth, and seventeenth centuries bears a remarkable resemblance to what the profession knows today as "communicative language teaching." In a highly readable account of second language research findings, Lightbown and Spada (1993) offer the following distinguishing characteristics of the communicative classroom:

Emphasis is placed on the meaning conveyed by a message rather than on its surface form;

A limited amount of error correction is exercised;

Language is made comprehensible to learners by the use of context and extralinguistic cues, rather than by structural grading of forms;

Students are exposed to a variety of discourse types;

Students' errors are considered a natural part of the learning process and little pressure is applied to perform at high levels of accuracy; and,

Teachers are encouraged to adapt their language to maximize learners' understanding (Lightbown & Spada, pp. 72-73).

The features of a theoretically sound language learning environment, therefore, appear to have changed little over the centuries. However, it is important to keep in mind that the Lightbown and Spada text is not a pedagogical manual; it is a presentation of current research in second language acquisition. Although they support communicative language teaching theory in light of that research, these authors do not offer specific recommendations for teaching practice. The history of the evolution of theory into practice in second language teaching begs the question of whether the tenets of communicative language teaching theory are, in fact, conveyed in teaching manuals.

Despite the similarity between the description of communicative language teaching by Lightbown and Spada and the reforms advocated throughout the history of language teaching, current pedagogical manuals hesitate to claim allegiance to any one approach to pedagogy.

In a book entitled *Making Communicative Language Teaching Happen*, which does present a consistent theoretical framework for classroom practice based on psycholinguistic research, the authors state in the introduction that "this book is also different because it is not the product of a particular theory, method, or school of thought" (Lee & VanPatten 1995, p. x). The danger that arises from not making the underlying theoretical stance clear is that eclecticism, even "informed eclecticism" (as proposed by Richards & Rodgers 1986, p. 158 and Brown 1993, p. 15), is by its definition a hodgepodge.

The failure of audiolingualism has put many methodologists on guard. Some go so far as to actively promote a hybrid approach to language teaching:

> The instructor "borrows" from communicative approaches the basic theoretical and philosophical perspectives, uses a grammatical syllabus (instead of a functional one, which some communicative approaches would suggest), and treats the subject matter using humanistic techniques that have been suggested in yet another type of approach (Omaggio 1986, p. 44).

Despite good intentions in the presentation of a multiplicity of approaches and techniques, tempered with the admonishment that teachers select the "best" from among them, such open-ended acceptance of components fails to ensure the compatibility of the parts that constitute the resulting harlequinesque plan. Teachers are encouraged to use "the best" of our "accumulated knowledge" and "what works," but how are they to make that selection unless they have some evidence of effectiveness?

Because proficiency-oriented instruction currently enjoys a high profile in language teaching, a closer examination of the actual pedagogy that is advocated in the proficiency-oriented classroom is necessary. Such investigation reveals that, once again, confusing guidelines and contradictory statements obscure reform.

Rather than a prescribed method, proficiency-oriented instruction offers "hypotheses" and "corollaries" to inform a classroom practice designed to create fluent users of the second language. The first hypothesis maintains that students must practice the language in a wide range of contexts to develop functional competence. Four corollaries derive from this hypothesis:

Corollary 1. Students should be encouraged to express their own meaning as early as possible after productive skills have been introduced in the course of instruction;

Corollary 2. Opportunities must be provided for active communicative interaction among students;

Corollary 3. Creative language practice (as opposed to exclusively manipulative or convergent practice) must be encouraged in the proficiency-oriented classroom; and,

Corollary 4. Authentic language should be used in instruction wherever possible (Omaggio Hadley 1993, pp. 80-82).

The reader would be correct in the assumption that all of these corollaries are supported by proponents of communicative language teaching (with the elimination of the stipulation of "wherever possible" in corollary 4); however, a closer look at the actual recommendations for classroom practice demonstrate that the transmission of theory into practice remains contentional.

With regard to the use of authentic language (corollary 4), the author advises "we might obtain the best results by using simplified versions of authentic materials with Novice and Intermediate-Level students and moving gradually toward incorporating more complete, unedited language samples with Advanced-Level learners" (p. 82). Aside from the obvious fact that when the texts are simplified they are no longer authentic, the insistence on delaying the use of authentic texts to more advanced levels of language learners is a feature, not of the reformers' stance, but of the status quo. Although the author does tentatively suggest that "we might also consider providing enough extralinguistic cues to render unedited authentic materials comprehensible to Novice- or Intermediate-level students" (p. 82), later examples of how to use authentic readings are geared almost entirely toward higher levels of proficiency. The notion that it is the learners' level of grammatical knowledge that ultimately determines their interaction with authentic text, rather than their interpretive ability based on myriad factors, leads the author to conclude that "whether material is edited or not, it is important to choose input that is appropriate in form and content to the student's current level of proficiency" (p. 82). This is very different from the stance taken by the education reformers whose only concern was that the content of the material be appropriate to students' *age*, not the number of years they had studied the language.

Likewise, the first and the third corollaries of the hypothesis are called into question when, in the first edition of the text, the reader is admonished *not* to encourage learners' creative use of the language:

> There appears to be a real danger of leading students too rapidly into the "creative aspects of language use," in that if successful communication is encouraged and regarded for its own sake, the effect seems to be one of rewarding at the same time the *incorrect* communication strategies seized upon in attempting to deal with the communication situations presented. When these reinforced communication strategies fossilize prematurely, their subsequent modification or ultimate correction is rendered difficult to the point of impossibility (Higgs & Clifford 1982, p. 74; cited in Omaggio 1986, p. 33).

The fear of allowing students to make mistakes in the second language pervades the pedagogy. The insistence on accuracy is not a hidden agenda, but a core feature of the pedagogical orientation. The avoidance of linguistic errors from the beginning is confirmed by the third hypothesis of proficiency-oriented instruction:

> The development of accuracy should be encouraged in proficiency-oriented instruction. As learners produce language, various forms of instruction and evaluative feedback can be useful in facilitating the progression of their skills toward more precise and coherent language use (Omaggio Hadley 1993, p. 83).

What makes the discussion of accuracy so confusing, however, is not that error correction forms an integral part of the approach (a cornerstone of Battista's treatise and the *Ratio*), rather it is the contradiction that arises in the pedagogical directives. On the one hand, the author maintains that:

> Attention to accuracy does not imply a classroom environment where grammar rules reign supreme and correction is rigidly imposed. Rather, the proficiency-oriented classroom is one in which students have ample opportunities to use language creatively and to obtain appropriate feedback with which they can progressively build and refine their interlanguage to approximate the target language norm. This feedback is provided in an atmosphere characterized by acceptance of error as a necessary condition for linguistic growth, an atmosphere in which the teacher is seen as a valuable resource in the language-learning process (p. 283).

On the other hand, the sample lesson plan provided in the manual suggests that the lesson is designed around the accurate manipulation of a particular grammar point, in this case "the use of the indefinite article in negative sentences:"

> 9:00-9:05   Warmup activity. The teacher reviews the previous day's work by asking students to describe their rooms in a simple question-answer exchange. The teacher asks various people in the class if they have certain objects in their rooms, what color their rooms are, and what sorts of things they like to do in their rooms. The teacher follows up each initial question to a given student with two or three related questions, creating the feeling of a conversation rather than an interrogation (p. 491).

The teacher is warned that the exchange must be manipulated in such a way as to simulate a conversation, a difficult task to accomplish given that the teacher is the only one who asks questions and the students are called upon to provide answers that do not further the conversation. Following the warm up, the real lesson begins:

> 9:05-9:10   Introduction of the grammatical structure. The teacher asks students to turn to a page in their text (Muskens et al. 1982, p. 85), where a short description of a student's dorm room is given. A drawing shows a student looking in a bewildered fashion around his new living quarters near the university. In this description, students are introduced to negative sentences as follows:
> Il y a une lampe, mais pas d'électricité.
> (There is a lamp, but no electricity.)
> Il y a un lavabo, mais pas d'eau chaude.
> (There is a sink, but no water.)
> Students are asked to complete similar sentences about the room, looking at another illustration. For example, they can see that there is a table, but no chair, a bookcase, but no books, and so forth. In this way, they show that they understand the negative construction through their active use of it in a simple exercise (Omaggio Hadley, p. 492).

The purpose of the students' communication is to relate in the second language what everyone can already see on the page of the textbook. Because the content of the messages is already known to all the participants, no meaningful exchange of information occurs with this activity. No authentic second language text is used either because language is presented at only the sentence level. Instead, as the author clearly states, the goal of the exercise is the correct use of negative construction. During the next stage of the lesson, students must explain the grammatical rule:

> 9:10-9:15   Students explanation of the grammatical principle. The teacher then asks students to explain how the negative sentences they have just created are different from the affirmative ones. As students attempt to give a rule, the teacher can see if they have understood the concept. (Because students formulate the rule after seeing various examples of the structure in use, this type of presentation represents an inductive approach to the teaching of grammar.) If students seem to have understood the concept, the rest of the class time is spent in active practice, both oral and written. If they have not understood, the teacher gives a concise explanation, using the sentences just practiced as an illustration. (This second phase of the explanation, if necessary, represents a deductive approach, since the teacher first explains the rule and then illustrates it with examples) (pp. 492-493).

Although earlier the author asserted that proficiency-oriented instruction does not place undue emphasis on the learning of grammatical rules, the above recommendation for classroom practice suggests otherwise. Ironically, recent research has confirmed what the educational reformers have long known, that the ability to state a grammatical rule does not signify that a learner can use the rule in communicative situations (Lightbown 1985). Having formulated, either inductively or deductively, the grammatical rule, the lesson moves into the "active" phase:

> 9:15-9:35   Active practice: oral. Students work through a variety of contextualized exercises in the text, practicing the new negative construction while describing various scenes in the dorm, in the classroom, on campus, and in the town. Some of these exercises are done in a whole-class format, while others are done with students working together in pairs. The teacher circulates to help and explain, based on individual needs. It is during this phase of the lesson that students who are still unsure about how the concept works can ask specific questions. The teacher can also listen carefully to see if students are using the new structure appropriately, thereby verifying that they have understood the concept. If many students seem to be confused about the same exercise or are making similar mistakes, the teacher may want to interrupt the practice briefly to explain the concept further. Or the teacher may provide a correct model of the exercise in question and have the students repeat accordingly (Omaggio Hadley, p. 492).

In this segment of the lesson as well, the students' use of the second language is limited to conveying meanings that have been predesignated in the text-book exercises; no new or unknown information is exchanged. Although the information may be "contextualized" in terms of the lesson's theme, "student housing," because they are not acquiring subject-matter knowledge, the students are not held responsible for remembering the information presented. Once again, discourse is limited to the sentence-level, and the overriding concern for linguistic accuracy is apparent: The teacher circulates to detect and correct errors. The last directive in this stage appears to support the use of pattern repetition. The pedagogy still equates "understanding the grammatical concept" with the ability to use the structure in communicative situations. It does not take into consideration that the acquisition of certain grammatical structures emerges gradually and in developmentally-ordered sequences, regardless of when they were "taught" in the curriculum.

The second part of the active practice (9:35-9:42) is written and consists of a dictation that includes the grammatical structure just practiced, along with immediate correction either by comparison against the model text or by the teacher.

Finally, the remaining eight minutes of the class period are spent on "conversational practice:"

> 9:42-9:50   Conversational practice. Students use conversation cards to ask and answer personalized questions, many of which will require negative responses. In this manner, they finish the hour in group practice, actively engaged in using the new grammatical concept in an open-ended exchange (p. 493).

The concluding statement would lead the teacher to believe that an apparently smooth transition has taken (or should have taken) place, from the introduction of a specific grammar point to its correct use by students actively engaged in real communication. In terms of second language acquisition, what does it mean that students have "used the grammatical concept?" Is the negative construction now a permanent part of their linguistic repertoires? To answer that question, one would need to assess learners' use of the structure on a variety of occasions, in various instances of actual communication, and certainly at a longer interval than forty minutes from its formal presentation in the language classroom. More important, given the requisite language use in second language learning, have these students even been "actively engaged [...] in an open-ended exchange"?

"Conversation cards," the culminating activity, are promoted as a means to achieve "a blend of communication with a concern for accuracy" (p. 258). The technique works as follows: Students are divided into groups of three and within each group each student receives one card. On two of the cards are questions to ask one's conversation partner. For example, Card 1 may contain the following statements, written in the students' native language and requiring formulation in the second language: "Ask your partner where he/she plans to go this summer, how long he/she will stay, whether he/she will travel by car, plane, or train, or whom he/she will travel with. The student holding Card 2 has the following list: "Ask your partner whether he/she plans to travel one day to a German-speaking country, what country or countries he/she prefers to visit, what cities he/she would like to see, or how long he/she would like to stay in Germany." The third student does not take part in the exchange, rather this student plays the role of corrector. Card 3 contains the following instructions:

> Help your classmates ask their interview questions by using the cues below. Be careful to correct your partners when necessary, but be flexible and accept any correct form of the questions. Take notes on the answers you hear so you can report back the discussion to the rest of the class (All references to the content of "conversation cards" are from Omaggio Hadley, 1993, p. 259).

Card 3 also lists in the second language the questions that students 1 and 2 should ask.

The use of "conversation cards" does not produce anything resembling true conversation (Kinginger 1990). Instead, the two "conversation" partners routinely subvert the exercise into a translation task whose goal becomes the accurate conversion of the native language statements into second language questions. The third student typically takes on the role of the enforcer.

The analysis of the one detailed lesson plan included in a manual for proficiency-oriented instruction is not meant to suggest that advocates of the approach recommend that each and every lesson be conducted according to such a fixed timetable. The author proposes that the following day's activities include some cultural information in the form of a lecture and slide presentation about student housing in France; the fact that the lesson still remains grammar-driven is obvious in her statement that "students will then comment on the slides in the target language, *using the new negative construction in their description* where appropriate" (Omaggio Hadley, 1993, p. 493, emphasis mine). The introduction to the manual indicates that "The model that unfolds in the pages of this book represents *one* interpretation of our accumulated knowledge about the way people learn languages in classrooms. It is not meant to be prescriptive" (p. xii). Yet, by presenting this lesson plan in the last chapter entitled "Planning Instruction for the Proficiency-Oriented Classroom: Some Practical Guidelines," it is difficult to see how this pedagogy differs in any significant way from the form-focused guidelines of Battista, or how it is any less rigidly prescriptive than the *Ratio*.

Unlike eclectic methods that preempt the careful examination of the relationship between classroom practice and learning outcomes, content-based instruction—in which the second language is used as the medium of communication for subject matter learning—provides the most well-documented evidence of the second language pedagogy that consistently achieves the goal of producing competent users of the L2. It is also the approach that most closely resembles the stance taken by the historical reformers: All instruction takes place in the L2; interesting texts are used extensively; and the second language is used primarily to interpret and express meaning, not as the object of study in and of itself. Although it is true that the students who emerge from content-based programs are not entirely nativelike in their expressive skills, they are indistinguishable from native speakers on interpretive tasks and they consistently outperform learners from all other instructional environments (Swain, 1985). Research is ongoing to discover how to further improve learning outcomes. Despite its proved success, content-based instruction has not been widely accepted by the teaching profession. The programs that do exist remain relegated largely to the elementary school, with a few notable exceptions. Krueger & Ryan (1992) provide an overview of current initiatives in content-based instruction at the postsecondary level.

Pause to consider . . .

that language practitioners, burned by the failure of audiolingualism, are often warned against "jumping on the bandwagon" of every new method or technique that comes along. Given the dual traditions throughout the history of second language teaching, is it even possible to identify what might constitute a professional "bandwagon?" What else may still prevent methodologists from abandoning a grammar-driven syllabus?

HOW INNOVATION HAPPENS
(OR: WHAT HAPPENS TO INNOVATION)

In 1994, during a panel presentation on the future of second language teaching, several well-known applied linguists from a large research institution offered their opinions on the directions language teaching would take. All the panelists were professors whose academic responsibilities also included language program direction: in Spanish, French, Italian, and English as an International Language. The audience consisted of graduate students in second language studies and faculty from related disciplines across campus: psychology, formal linguistics, and literature. One researcher proposed that no lasting curricular changes would occur until the professional and academic preparation of applied linguistics in charge of such programs was recognized and valued by the institution. Another observed that much more qualitative classroom-based research needs to be done to assess whether programs that purport to be "communicative" according to the course syllabi and daily activities actually engage students in meaningful language use. The methodologist among them proclaimed that the paradigm shift in second language teaching—from the grammatical curriculum with its insistence on the form-focused drill, accuracy and error correction to the communicative classroom in which the second language is used to interpret and express meaning—was finally complete. She stated perfunctorily, "Today, everyone teaches communicatively." The other panelists, also well-versed in classroom interaction research and intimately involved in teacher education, were visibly surprised. How could two such divergent interpretations of the status quo coexist? The methodologist in the previous incident is not alone in such a rosy assessment of current pedagogy. Ellis (1990), too, claims that "since the mid-seventies there have been considerable changes in second and foreign language teaching, accompanied by intensive debate about syllabus design, materials, and classroom practice" (p. 26).

One must be careful, however, not to be lulled into thinking that innovations have been implemented simply because they have been widely discussed in professional journals or new materials have been produced. Fullan (1992), who studies educational change and how it does (or doesn't) happen in institutionalized settings, warns:

> Without continuous monitoring of what is happening locally, we [proponents of reform] sail off, very quickly, into Wonderland. Teachers are then often obliged to feed selective, self-protective information to administrators who are now transmitting good news to the outside world and cannot contend with bad news from within (p. 9).

Have the changes advocated by both history and current theory become established practice in actual classrooms where the goal of instruction is to develop learners' functional competence?

Three educational reformers, Guarino, Ignatius, and Comenius, are hallowed in the annals of history for the innovations that they introduced into Western education: the study of humanities, the organization and administration of schools, and the use of illustrations in textbooks. Despite the continued endurance of those innovations, the connection between them and the teaching of a second language has become obscured. Viewed solely from a present-day perspective, it appears as though the changes in curriculum, administration, and materials occurred spontaneously and without context. Deeper exploration of the educators' works revealed that nothing could be further from the truth. In each instance, *the proposed innovation was optimally designed to promote the learning of a second language*, with the development of interpretive and expressive abilities in learners as its primary goal. How is it possible that all three reformers could hold nearly identical beliefs about second language acquisition, and yet that none of these beliefs has become institutionalized to the extent that the other, more superficial, innovations had been?

The reader may assume that theory fails to be transmitted in practice because it is untenable in the face of real world data, that is, in actual class-rooms where teachers and students go about the daily business of language learning. Modern observers of educational innovation remind us that the enactment of fundamental change is a messy and difficult endeavor (Fullan 1992, 1993; Huberman & Miles 1984; Rudduck 1992). Moreover, it would be too simplistic and historically inaccurate to assume that the best pedagogy does *ipso facto* and in all instances prevail:

> We come out, then, with intriguing paradoxes. That smooth initial implementation is usually a sign of trivial change. That problems of initial sacrifices *elsewhere* (less time for mathematics, more confusing transitions or scheduling, contradictory evaluation criteria) are in fact signs that significant changes are being enacted. That rapid success can lead, very quickly, to rapid decline (key people leave or turn their attention elsewhere, replaced by others with lesser credentials or another agenda). *That there is no necessary relationship between the proven success of an innovation—even in terms of increments in pupils' achievement or capacities—and its longevity* (Huberman in his "Intro-duction" to Fullan, 1992, p. 6; latter emphasis mine).

As argued previously, the methodologies proposed by Battista, the *Ratio Studiorum*, and parts of Comenius's *Great Didactic*, do not represent the practical application of the reformers' theories. Neither do the directives for profi-ciency-oriented instruction represent "the basic theoretical and philosophical perspectives" of communicative language teaching theory. On the contrary, they reflect an entirely different approach to second language education, even a contradictory one with respect to the original proposals. Within this opposing view, language learning is seen as the accomplishment of a series of steps progressing from simple to complex grammatical constructions instilled in learners through rules, drills, repetition, and correction. Because it reinforces rather than challenges established practices, this latter view does not disrupt the status quo of the institutional setting; therefore, it does not instigate or support reform. Under these circumstances, rather than intro-duce successful new practices quite the opposite can occur. The work of Huberman and others on the institutionalization of innovation reveals the following:

> As noted earlier, proven and acknowledged success is usually a nec-essary but by no means a sufficient requirement for institutionaliza-tion. Our research, along with Robert Yin's has shown that, under certain conditions, dismal projects can be institutionalized and highly successful ones can be buried (Huberman & Miles 1984; Yin & White 1984 cited in Fullan 1992, pp. 10-11).

The pedagogical directives advocated concurrently by Guarino, Ignatius, and Comenius did not fail to become institutionalized because they could not succeed. These were not "pie in the sky" ideas proposed by impractical theorists without application to actual classrooms. Instead, they represented successful instantiations of theory into practice which the reformers themselves experienced, but which nevertheless failed to become institutionalized. Why?

In his book, *Successful School Improvement: The Implementation Perspective and Beyond*, Fullan (1992) relates the results of research intended to "uncover the many layers of complexity" in the process of enacting changes in instructional practice (p. vii). Based on his and others' investigations into how educational reforms are realized in institutional settings, Fullan creates a tripartite model of the requisites for successful implementation of instructional innovations. In the theoretical model, he proposes that changes in three areas (i.e., methods, materials, and beliefs) are central to the successful implementation of innovation in schools. He also laments the fact that the database on which his model is founded rests on only thirty years' evidence! It would seem that a diachronic perspective on second language education could contribute to the cogency of Fullan's model, as a clearer picture of the relative contributions of each criteria emerges in light of the historical evidence.

First, in reference to changes in methods, the *Ratio Studiorum* reveals the detrimental effect that the removal of the theoretical stance—the rationalization behind the prescription—has on teaching manuals. Devoid of its theoretical underpinnings, instructional practice is reduced to a compendium of rules to be followed, rendered arbitrary and suffocatingly rigid in the process. Such prescriptivism may pervade the subject matter itself, as it did in the study of Latin in the *Ratio*, reducing it to a series of structures to be slavishly memorized and repeated ad nauseam. Total immersion in the second language, as one example, becomes in such a context a burden that hapless students must bear for fear of persecution by linguistic spies, rather than the *lingua franca* of a community of scholars.

Providing teachers with a list of rules to follow, no matter how detailed, does not grant the understanding they need to make informed choices about practice. Instead, the *Ratio* projects a lucid historical example of "the programmatic approach that often falsely assumes that attempts to change how people think through mission statements or training programs will lead to useful changes in how people actually behave at work" (Beer, Eisenstat & Spector 1990, p. 150). Method, without theory, does not ensure innovation. "The more that you 'tighten' mandates," Fullan (1993) argues, "the more that educational goals and means get narrowed, and consequently the less impact there is" (p. 23). Mandates may alter the external perception of things, giving the illusion of change, but "they do not affect what matters. When complex change is involved, people do not and cannot change by being told to do so" (p. 24).

Although it is true that in the English-as-a-Second-Language context, instruction tends to be conducted exclusively in the second language—more a function of the linguistically diverse student population than for any theoretical coherence—the same is not true in many, if not most, foreign language classrooms. There, the students' shared first language is depended upon to convey ideas more quickly and easily than they could be in the second language, or as a check to make sure that students have truly understood a message conveyed in the second language. Such attempts may appear to render instruction more efficient when, in fact, they thwart the learners' need to develop interpretive competence in the second language; the simultaneous translations advocated in the *Ratio* or the popular interlinear translations of Latin texts produced similar results. Moreover, reform that expects an exclusive use of the second language as the medium for all classroom interaction must also address the not too uncommon situation in which the second language competence of the teacher is insufficient to maintain the exclusive use of the second language.

The fact that instruction occurs in the second language does not guarantee that the focus of such instruction is on the communication of messages. For example, a newly graduated language teacher who had learned in a methods course the importance of incorporating opportunities for personalized language use into her lessons later reported to her former professor that her secondary school students studying Spanish didn't like those activities. When questioned further, she explained how she had asked her students to list their three favorite activities on a sheet of paper and hand them in. The next day, she returned the papers, all marked "wrong," because the students had failed to state their answers in complete and grammatically accurate sentences. From that day on, the students refused to engage any further in "personalized" exercises. Clearly, method is important only to the extent that teachers understand the principles of language learning that underscore it.

No one was a more firm believer in method than Comenius, in spite of the fact that he believed teachers themselves had no need to study methods. In his view, materials—the second of Fullan's criteria for change—were a necessary and sufficient condition for the reform of second language teaching practice. Here too, however, the historical perspective reveals the distortion that materials undergo in the process of marketing and large-scale adoption by teachers who do not share the theoretical framework in which the materials were created. The adopters of Comenius's textbooks found them too difficult for use at the elementary level for which they were intended, and they clamored for a revision of the materials to reflect the prevailing, institutionalized beliefs about language learning and teaching. The reformers' insistence that learners can comprehend the second language and acquire content area knowledge in it before they "master" all of its grammatical complexities, central to the innovation, was not and could not be conveyed in the materials themselves.

Today the role that materials play in fostering change remains suspect. A perusal of current second and foreign language textbooks suffices to reveal a continuing reliance on a grammatical syllabus to structure textbooks. Language learning objectives remain stated in terms of the structures that learners will be able to manipulate at the end of a specific period of instruction with little regard for developmental orders of acquisition or the transitory nature of instructional effects. Ironically, even the existence of theoretically sound materials no more ensures their appropriate use in today's second language classroom than they did in Comenius's time, as illustrated by the following example.

An applied linguist recently gave a workshop on the value of using authentic second language texts in the classroom. He chose to illustrate his point with a reading found in an introductory-level Spanish text written by a team of second language acquisition specialists, including an expert in second language reading research. As he began the workshop, one of the participants eagerly offered that, not only did she already use authentic texts in her teaching, she had adopted the very same textbook in one of her courses. Thinking he could rely on the participant's practical experience to prove his point, the workshop director asked the teacher to describe how she introduced a particular reading entitled "¿Funcionas mejor de día o de noche?" [Do you function better in the morning or at night?]. The teacher replied that first she directs the learners' attention to the title of the reading. At this point the presenter smiled, certain that next the teacher would ask the students to hypothesize, from the title, the text's content. The teacher then explained that she repeats the title of the article to the class "¿Tú funcionas mejor de día o de noche?" [You, do you function better in the morning or at night?]. Then, to one student she asks, ¿y ella? [And she?] to which the student must reply ¿Ella funciona mejor de día o de noche? [Does she function better in the morning or at night?] To another, she asks ¿y Ustedes? [And you all] to receive the response ¿Ustedes funcionan mejor de día o de noche? [Do you all function better in the morning or at night?]. She continues in this manner until all the subject pronouns have been represented. Unmercifully, the teacher had transformed the reading of an authentic text into a pattern drill.

When the applied linguist recounted this episode to me, he was appalled that someone had so completely misconstrued the theory of second language reading that pervades this textbook. I, instead, was delighted, not because the incident occurred, but because it presents an outstanding contemporary example of why innovations in materials—even materials that are carefully constructed by experts in second language acquisition theory—are not a sufficient means to instigate a change in the behavior of language teachers. True and lasting innovation, according to Fullan, requires the modification of teachers' beliefs. The introduction of new materials, being concrete and tangible and more susceptible to revision by theorists, may be the easiest features of the curriculum to manipulate, but they are not reliable change agents themselves.

There is yet another way in which current "communicative" materials do not reflect the original intent of the language reformers. Language teaching is communicative in so far as it insists on the centrality of the interpretation, expression, and negotiation of meaning to the acquisition process. The content and language connection that formed the basis of the *studia humanitatis* is lost, however, when students learn only to communicate personal needs and never investigate levels of meaning beyond that which is readily apparent on the surface or avoid discussion of new or controversial ideas that challenge their thinking and not merely their linguistic ability in a second language. Immersion education research provides overwhelming evidence to support the link between the acquisition of language and subject matter knowledge. The current interest in content-based instruction reflects the continued attempt, begun centuries ago, to re-establish that link. It seems impossible that middle-school-aged European children in the fifteenth through seventeenth centuries were more capable of dealing with intellectually challenging subject matter than many university students today. However, the implementation of such a change would challenge the institutional confines that currently separate so-called "language" courses from the rest of the curriculum.

The popularity of a profusion of new textbooks promoting "communicative" activities or "proficiency-oriented instruction" may lull the profession into believing that actual change in teaching practice has occurred. Especially when viewed in conjunction with an "eclectic" pedagogy, in which teachers pick-and-choose freely among various pedagogical options, the ease with which innovation is implemented can be a warning sign, rather than a cause for rejoicing:

> One of the dangers of complex innovations is that implementors may develop a sense of false clarity if they only incorporate the easy to learn features of the innovation into their practice. Or if the change is experienced to be complex and overwhelming without substantial progress, users often give up, 'down-size' or trivialize the change (Huberman & Miles 1984).

A 1995 survey accompanying the proposal of a new foreign language textbook provides an example of such trivialization of language teaching reform. The questionnaire posed the following questions to prospective adopters of the book: "Where would you like to see pattern drills?" "Should the grammar explanation appear at the beginning, in the middle or at the end of the chapter?" "Which method do you use: communicative (students work in pairs and groups); proficiency-based (grammar is used as a reference); traditional (grammar is the focus)?" "How important are the following: grammar explanations, dialogs, pattern practice, realia, color photos, culture?" When textbook authors, publishers, and teachers assume that pattern drills and grammar explanations are essential features of a language textbook, or when they reduce communicative language teaching to "students work in pairs and groups," and equate the contribution of culture to that of dialogs and color photos, one should not be surprised that materials fail to promote a more theoretically-informed approach to second language teaching.

The last issue raised by Guarino, Ignatius, and Comenius and seconded by current psycholinguistic research, namely, that second language learners progress differentially in their rate of acquisition, presents a complex problem for both curriculum design and evaluation. Learners attended Guarino's school until their second language skills were sufficient to meet the linguistic demands of their chosen professions. Similarly, Ignatius's proposal specified that learners proceed through the curriculum at a rate commensurate with their ability to meet instructional objectives. Given that students move through albeit predictable sequences of acquisition, but at varying and unpredictable rates, what constitutes "sufficient" progress for a student who has completed an elementary course in French, Portuguese, or Japanese? What is "outstanding" progress? If the difference between the two were an artifact of individual variation outside the learners' conscious control, would it be fair to assign a grade of "C" to the former and an "A" to the latter? Because Guarino's and many of Ignatius's students were native speakers of a language derived from Latin it is reasonable to assume that the similarities between the learners' first and second languages facilitated acquisition of the latter, at least with respect to rate of progress. In today's language courses, are the experienced language learners, for example, the ones who are acquiring a second or third Romance language, to be evaluated according to the same criteria as the students who are attempting to learn such a language for the first time? Moreover, if students' linguistic progress reaches a plateau in the second or third year of classroom instruction, how can such progress be assigned a letter grade at the end of the semester? Applied linguists are just beginning to address these issues. In a research article about the value of journal writing in second language instruction, Casanave (1994) offers an alternative framework for the evaluation of students' progress in just such a linguistically stabilized situation.

*P*ause to consider . . .

that assessing achievement in a second language remains a controversial issue. When language and content area instruction proceed hand-in-hand, then subject-matter testing conducted in the second language provides a natural, but "academic" context for evaluation. How does the separation of language and content confound the testing of students' communicative ability?

BREAKING TRADITION: WHAT'S AT RISK?

When the reformers, past and present, are taken seriously in their attempts to change beliefs, and thereby practices, about second language learning and teaching, the consequences for educational institutions are many and complex. This is as it should be. Sizer (1991) sums up the situation succinctly when he admits that although he initially believed that change should proceed slowly and cautiously, he now understands that a more aggressive posture is required:

> In a school, everything important touches everything else of importance. Change one consequential aspect of that school and all others will be affected. [...] We are stuck with a school reform game in which any change affects all, where everyone must change if anything is to change (p. 32).

Faced with such challenging and complex issues, where does one begin? The historical evidence and modern thought on how change happens concur that the creation of new materials and methods is insufficient. Rather, the second language teaching profession must effect a decisive change in beliefs about how second languages are learned.

---

*P*ause to consider . . .

if, according to Sizer, all important aspects of the curriculum are deeply interdependent, then what would be the impact of a decision to teach completely and solely in the second language from the first day of the first course? How would it affect the students? The teachers? What would be the repercussions to upper division courses and their faculty?

Of what use to today's language professionals is an acquaintance with language teaching theories of educational reformers whose beliefs about second language learning and teaching failed to be transmitted even within their own epochs? They point to the centrality of Fullan's third criterion for successful implementation of reform: changes in beliefs. Fullan emphasizes the importance of this factor when he states that "dealing with innovation effectively means alterations in *behaviours* and *beliefs*" (1992, p. 22). In his later work (1993), he underscores the overriding exigency of changing beliefs, claiming that "it is no denial of the potential worth of particular innovations to observe that unless deeper changes in thinking and skills occur there will be limited impact" (p. 23).

The historical evidence unequivocally and powerfully confirms the imperative of conveying the theoretical framework that supports the use of particular methodologies and materials to the language practitioner. It is precisely in this arena where the historical reformers failed. None of the documents destined to transmit their innovations to future generations reflected the fundamental change in beliefs that regards language as a system of communication, and second language acquisition as a developmental process during which learners must engage in the interpretation and expression of meaning. The complexity of the issues involved points to the education of an even wider audience, one that includes everyone who has an interest in language education: teachers, students, administrators, business, and the general public. Fullan most appropriately concludes, "Teacher education still has the honour of being simultaneously the worst problem and the best solution in education" (1993, p. 105). To whom does the responsibility for providing this education ultimately fall? The applied linguists.

The diachronic perspective on second language teaching afforded by this study confirms that the impetus for change can only come from those who have a thorough grounding in theory and whose research takes them into classrooms where real learners and teachers create meaning in the second language. Modern applied linguists affirm the importance of a "focus on integrating theory and practice in [second language] teacher education" (Richards & Nunan 1990, p. 41). Second language education textbooks in which theory and practice are presented in tandem contribute to that effort.

Those who insist on the "traditional" second language teaching methods of Battista, the *Ratio*, and Comenius because they have always been around are at least historically naive. However, to continue to perpetuate such myths is destructive to second language learners, teachers, and programs because they doom all to failure. The historical evidence demonstrates that educators with vision have always known the ineffectiveness of classroom practices that persist in using the L1 as the language of instruction, insist on the explicit teaching of grammatical rules, engage students in drill and repetition, and delay subject matter instruction and extensive use of authentic texts until late in the curricular sequence; despite their longevity, these methods were never effective in developing communicative competence in learners.

In 1983, Stern advocated the need for historical analyses to examine second language teaching within its wider historical, social, and political context. Yet, in one of his last articles, published posthumously in 1990, he states, "Language teaching methods in the past have always been mainly analytic, in the sense that they have based themselves on some kind of analysis of the language, with an emphasis on grammar" (p. 94). The examination of three centuries of the profession's past denies Stern's pessimistic assessment. It is only in the *transition* from theory to practice that the emphasis has routinely shifted from complex and experiential to straightforward and analytical. In breaking open second language teaching's past, a new tradition has emerged. Viewed from a historical perspective, innovation in second language teaching that is currently labeled "communicative" is not new in the absolute sense: It is only new to the institutional setting that has repeatedly failed to implement it with its original intent. The task of conveying theory into practice continues to challenge applied linguists. Shall we fare any better than our predecessors?

> ### *P*ause to consider . . .
>
> if there is a better way to convey theory into practice than through pedagogical manuals? How may current technology provide teachers with the opportunity to experience (and analyze) new approaches to language teaching?

A LOOK TO THE FUTURE

Only a century ago, no one imagined that a language could ever again attain the unprecedented sway that Latin once held over the world of scholarship, government, commerce, and international communication. Yet, today, the English language enjoys much the same status as Latin did during its heyday in the time of Guarino. Are we as confident in its perpetuality as the humanists were of Latin's? Will English become the language of wider communication for all, or will it be limited to an intellectual, political, or social elite? Will nationalistic interests once again impede the propagation of a truly universal language? If English were to eventually follow the route of Latin, first, as the language of an elite, later as a prestigious, but foreign, language of the middle class, and finally as an academic dinosaur, what would happen next? Like the generations who preceded us, we cannot begin to fathom what language may replace it. A computerized dialect of 0s and 1s perhaps? Future applied linguists, take note: There may be an interesting story to tell.

> *Mi fermai in questa sentenza: che*
> *qualunque modo di scrivere fosse meglio*
> *che, stando in ozio e in pigrizia, tacere.*
> *[I end with this: that any kind of writing*
> *is better than, in sloth and laziness, keep*
> *ing quiet.]*
> —Leonardo Bruni, Florentine History, 1400

References

Beer, M., Eisenstat, R. & Spector, B. (1990). *The critical path to corporate renewal*. Boston: Harvard Business School Press.

Boyd, W. (1966). *The history of western education*. New York: Barnes and Noble.

Brinton, D. M., Snow, M. A. & Wesche, M. B. (1989). *Content-based second language instruction*. New York: Newbury House.

Brown, H. D. (1994). *Principles of language learning and teaching*. Third edition. Englewood Cliffs, NJ: Prentice Hall Regents.

Brumfit, C. & Mitchell, R. (Eds.). (1990). *Research in the language classroom*. London: Modern English Publications in association with The British Council.

Casanave, C. P. (1994). Language development in students' journals. *Journal of second language writing, 3 (3)*, 179-201.

Cecchi, E. & Sapegno, N. (Eds.). (1966). *Storia della letteratura italiana*. Milan: Garzanti.

Chomsky, N. (1965). *Aspects of the theory of syntax*. Cambridge: M.I.T.

Cole, L. (1950). *A history of education: Socrates to Montessori*. New York: Holt, Rinehart and Winston.

Comenius, J. A. (1657). *Didactica magna*. [The great didactic]. In M. W. Keatinge. (Trans., Ed.) (1907). *The great didactic of John Amos Comenius*. Vol. 2. London: Adam and Charles Black.

Comenius, J. A. (1633). *Vestibulum. In Opera Didactica Magna*. Amsterdam.

Comenius, J. A. (1631). *Janua Linguarum Reserata. In Opera Didactica Magna*. Amsterdam.

Comenius, J. A. (1635). *De sermonis latini studio dissertatio. In Opera Didactica Magna*. Amsterdam.

Comenius, J. A. [facsimile of the third London edition 1672]. *Orbis sensualium pictus*. Sydney: Sydney University Press.

Diller, K. C. (1978). *The language teaching controversy*. Rowley, MA: Newbury House.

Ellis, R. (1990). Activities and procedures for teacher preparation. In J. Richards and D. Nunan. (Eds.), *Second language teacher education*. (pp. 26-36). Cambridge: Cambridge University Press.

Fitzpatrick, E. A. (Ed.). (1933). *St. Ignatius and the Ratio studiorum*. New York: McGraw-Hill.

Fullan, M. (1991). *The new meaning of educational change*. Toronto: Ontario Institute for Studies in Education.

Fullan, M. (1992). *Successful school improvement: The implementation perspective and beyond*. Philadelphia: Open University Press.

Fullan, M. (1993). *Change forces: Probing the depths of educational reform*. London: The Falmer Press.

Ganss, G. E. (1954). *Saint Ignatius' idea of a Jesuit university*. Milwaukee: The Marquette University Press.

Garin, E. (Ed.). (1958). *Il pensiero pedagogico dello Umanesimo*. Florence: Giuntine and Sansoni.

Guarini, B. *De ordine docendi et discendi*. In E. Garin. (Ed.). (1958). *Il pensiero pedagogico dello Umanesimo*. (pp. 434-471). Florence: Giuntine and Sansoni.

Guarini, G. *Le epistole di Guarino da Verona*. [The letters of Guarino da Verona.] In E. Garin. (Ed.). (1958). *Il pensiero pedagogico dello Umanesimo*. (pp. 306-433). Florence: Giuntine and Sansoni.

Huberman, A. M. & Miles, M. B. (1984). *Innovation up close: How school improvement works*. New York: Plenum.

Keatinge, M. W. (Trans., Ed.) (1907). *The great didactic of John Amos Comenius*. Vol. 2. London: Adam and Charles Black.

Keatinge, M. W. (Trans., Ed.) (1910). *The great didactic of John Amos Comenius*. Vol. 1. London: Adam and Charles Black.

Kelly, L. G. (1969). *25 Centuries of language teaching*. Rowley, MA: Newbury House.

Kinginger, C. (1990). *Task variation and classroom learner discourse*. Unpublished doctoral dissertation, University of Illinois at Urbana-Champaign.

Krueger, M. & Ryan, F. (1992). *Language and content: Discipline- and content-based approaches to language study*. Lexington, MA: D.C. Heath.

Lee, J. F. & VanPatten, B. (1995). *Making communicative language teaching happen*. New York: McGraw-Hill.

Lightbown, P. (1983). Exploring relationships between developmental and instructional sequences in L2 acquisition. In H. Seliger & M. Long. (Eds.). *Classroom-oriented research in second language acquisition*. (pp. 217-243). Rowley, MA: Newbury House.

Lightbown, P. & Spada, N. (1993). *How languages are learned*. London: Oxford University Press.

Loyola, Ignatius. [s.d.] The constitutions of the Society of Jesus. Part IV. In G. E. Ganss. (Trans., Ed.). (1954). *Saint Ignatius' idea of a Jesuit university*. (pp. 271-335). Milwaukee: The Marquette University Press.

Loyola, Ignatius. [s.d.] The constitutions of the Society of Jesus. Part IV. In E. A. Fitzpatrick. (Ed.) (1933). M. H. Mayer. (Trans.). *St. Ignatius and the Ratio studiorum*. (pp. 45-118). New York: McGraw-Hill.

Luther, M. (1524). Letter to the mayors and aldermen of all of cities of Germany in behalf of Christian schools. In R. Ulich. (Ed.). (1954). *Three thousand years of educational wisdom*. (pp. 218-238). Cambridge: Harvard University Press.

Luther, M. [s.d.]. Sermon on the duty of sending children to school. In R. Ulich. (Ed.). (1954). *Three thousand years of educational wisdom*. (pp. 238-249). Cambridge: Harvard University Press.

Mackey, W. F. (1965). *Language teaching analysis*. London: Longman.

Muskens, J., Omaggio, A., Chalmers, C., Imberton, C., & Amaras, P. (1982). *Rendez-vous*. New York: Random House.

Omaggio Hadley, A. (1993). *Teaching language in context*. Second edition. Boston: Heinle & Heinle.

Omaggio, A. (1986). *Teaching language in context*. Boston: Heinle & Heinle.

Ratio Studiorum of 1599. In E. A. Fitzpatrick. (Ed.) (1933). A. R. Ball. (Trans.). *St. Ignatius and the Ratio studiorum*. (pp. 119-254). New York: McGraw-Hill.

Richards, J. C. & Nunan, D. (Eds.). (1990). *Second language teacher education*. Cambridge: Cambridge University Press.

Richards, J. C. & Rodgers, T.S. (1986). *Approaches and methods in language teaching*. Cambridge: Cambridge University Press.

Rudduck, J. (1992). *Innovation and change: Developing involvement and understanding*. Philadelphia: Open University Press.

Savignon, S. J. (1983). *Communicative competence: Theory and classroom practice*. Reading, MA: Addison-Wesley.

Scaglione, A. (1986). *The liberal arts and the Jesuit college system*. Amsterdam: John Benjamins.

Sizer, T. (1991). No pain, no gain. *Educational leadership, 48, 8*, 32-34.

Stern, H. H. (1983). *Fundamental concepts of language teaching*. Oxford: Oxford University Press.

Swain, M. (1985). Communicative competence: Some roles of comprehensible input and comprehensible output in its development. In S. M. Gass & C. Madden. (Eds.). *Input in second language acquisition*. (pp. 235-253). Rowley, MA: Newbury House.

Titone, R. (1968). Teaching foreign languages: An historical sketch. Washington, DC: Georgetown University Press.

Vergerius, P. P. (1403). De ingenuis moribus et liberalis studiis. [On the conduct and education of young people]. In W. H. Woodward. (Trans., Ed.). (1921). *Vittorino da Feltre and other humanist educators*. (pp. 96-118). Cambridge: Cambridge University Press.

Yin, R. K. & White, J. L. (1984). *Microcomputer implementation in schools*. Washington, DC: COSMOS Corporation.

Young, W. J. (Trans., Ed.). (1959). *Letters of St. Ignatius of Loyola*. Chicago: Loyola University Press.

Index